"It's clear as soon as you crack the cover [that] [she's] left her heart somewhere beneath the Tro[pic] [of] [her] passion for the remarkably diverse spirits, peoples, and lands radiates from each page, and her book (and bar, Leyenda) are a testament to her desire to share them with us. Like the first sip of an ice-cold cocktail on a warm San Juan night, this book refreshes and delights."

—**MARTIN CATE**, author and owner of Smuggler's Cove, San Francisco

"Smartly written and beautifully photographed, *Spirits of Latin America* is a necessary addition to any thoughtful spirit lover's library. Ivy Mix goes far beyond technical insight and gets to the heart of what actually makes these spirits so special: the people who make them, the cultures from which they were born, and the lands that contribute so much to their personality. We're brought not just on a journey into her deep passion for agave, sugarcane, and grape spirits but are allowed to ride shotgun as Ivy explores the nuance of each, brings to life the voices of those who put their soul into every drop, and cultivates an appreciation for the deep heritage and tradition that are entwined with their stories."

—**ALEX DAY**, co-author of *Cocktail Codex: Fundamentals, Formulas, Evolutions* and *Death & Co: Modern Classic Cocktails*

"In this book, Ivy Mix reveals the roots of her inspiration: Latin American spirits, and her personal experience of the culture behind them. This book plumbs the depths—and provides a vivid portrait—of the spirits that have inspired cocktails that have taken the world by storm. You will not only get a first-class ticket to the places that have given birth to Latin American drink culture but exciting and easy to execute recipes that will appeal to home cocktail enthusiast and seasoned bar pro alike—Saludos!"

—**SHANNON MUSTIPHER**, beverage director of Glady's Caribbean, Brooklyn, and author of *Tiki: Modern Tropical Cocktails*

SPIRITS

OF LATIN AMERICA

SPIRITS

OF LATIN AMERICA

A CELEBRATION OF CULTURE & COCKTAILS, WITH 100 RECIPES FROM LEYENDA & BEYOND

IVY MIX

WITH JAMES CARPENTER

PHOTOGRAPHS BY SHANNON STURGIS

TEN SPEED PRESS
California | New York

FOR ESME

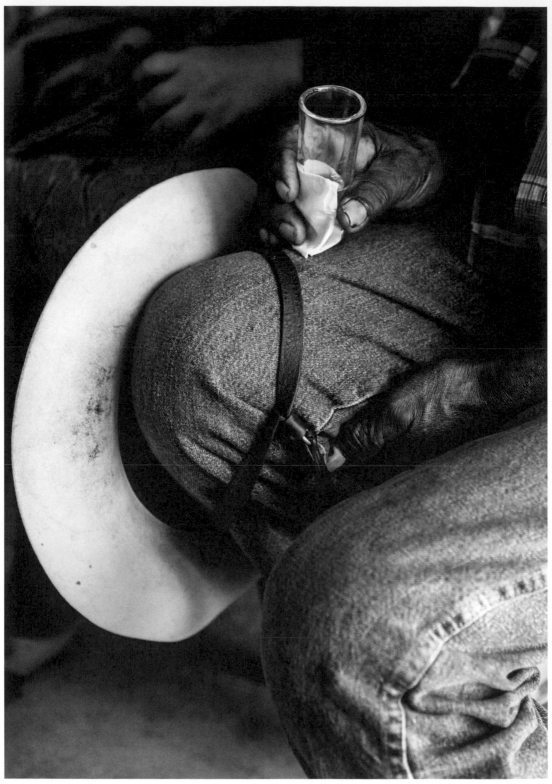

Above: Enjoying a mezcal in Candelaria de Yegolé, Oaxaca, Mexico. **Page ii:** Shrine to La Virgen de Guadalupe and Nuestra Señora de Juquila in the home of the Morales Luis family, who make mezcal in Santo Domingo Albarradas, Oaxaca, Mexico.

INTRODUCTION

> "It's a simple law of physics: energy doesn't die
> or go away, it has to be transmitted. It is through
> talking, dancing, and laughing that it is released.
> Latin spirits are the base for our celebration."
>
> —CARLOS CAMERENA, LA ALTEÑA DISTILLERY

I grew up in a very small town in central Vermont. By small, I mean *really* small—seven-hundred-people small—the type of town where everyone not only knows your name but they know everything about you, too. It was also far from cities or airports, so growing up, my experience of the big wide world was pretty limited.

When I decided to attend a liberal-arts college (again in Vermont), my life changed. The school year there was broken up into trimesters, and during the winter trimester each year, we were required to leave campus and complete study work in our field. I had zero idea what I wanted to do with myself or what my "field" would be—I just knew I wanted to go somewhere—*anywhere*—outside the country, learn a foreign language, and see something different from what I was used to. Though I didn't recognize it quite yet, I was suffering from a classic case of wanderlust.

I ended up in Antigua, Guatemala. A couple of days after I arrived, I stumbled into Antigua's now-famous Café No Sé, sat down, ordered a cerveza, and did my best to pretend that my nineteen-year-old self belonged in a bar. I enjoyed the place so much, I went back the next night—and every night thereafter for the whole two months I was in Antigua. When I returned to Vermont, I couldn't wait to turn around and go back again—which led to Guatemala being my home, and bartending my job, for about half of each year while I finished my degree. Whenever I was there, I spent my nights working and my days exploring, immersing myself in this foreign land that felt like home. Antigua is a particularly quaint little colonial town, and I would spend hours every day roaming the cobblestone streets and visiting the markets before I went to work.

Far from being cured by this experience, my wanderlust continued to grow. My travels began to take me to other parts of Latin America: first to Mexico with John, the owner of Café No Sé, to smuggle mezcal from Oaxaca back to Guatemala; then to Peru, followed by a stint in Argentina and beyond. Afterward, I moved to New York and began bartending there, finding ways and reasons to travel south whenever I could.

In 2015, I opened my bar, Leyenda, in Brooklyn—a bar dedicated to celebrating the Latin American cultures I'd fallen in love with. I'd been living in New York for seven years and was missing Latin America so much that I knew I was either going to have to move back down there or bring a little of *there* back to me. Leyenda was my solution—one way for me to bring my passion for bartending and my passion for Latin America together.

This book is another solution. Traveling south and getting to know Latin American people and their cultures, in part through what they drink, has taught me to relate to other people as a member of a global social society, rather than the island of one that I'd always felt before. With this book, I want to offer another context in which to do just that—to see ourselves as joined together with other cultures via their traditional spirits.

Many of the classic cocktails we know best come from Latin America— from the daiquiri to the margarita, the pisco sour to the Mojito. But in comparison with much of the rest of the world, Latin America doesn't have much of a cocktail culture to speak of. What it does have is a rich and vital tradition of spirits distillation.

Dry red soil in an agave field, La Alteña, Arandas, Jalisco, Mexico.

Farmer David William harvesting sugarcane in a freshly burnt field at the Appleton Estate, St. Elizabeth, Jamaica.

As a bartender who loves experimenting with flavor, I count the spirits of Latin America among my greatest inspirations; the cultural richness of these places is paralleled by the full, distinctive flavor of the spirits themselves. Spirits are like a palette of colors—you don't want one blue and one yellow to paint with; you want all of the shades within them. I want *big* flavors to create my drinks from; and to me, no other group of spirits has more life and vivaciousness and Technicolor flavor than that from Latin America. From the bright floral tints of Peruvian pisco to the earthy smokiness of Oaxacan mezcal, these are flavors that give me a *lot* to work with and can be made into some of the brightest, most vivid cocktails out there.

There's a word in wine culture that you've probably heard before: *terroir*. There is no direct English translation for this term, but it basically refers to the way geographic factors such as land, soil, topography, and climate impart flavors and other sensations to wine. I argue that terroir applies to all sorts of food and drink—and that it isn't just the land that affects the product, but also the identities, history, and culture of the places where foods and beverages come from. There are concrete reasons, both ecological and cultural, why Pinot Grigio ends up tasting different from, say, Verdejo, or why Chardonnay made in California tastes different from Chardonnay made in France. And there are also reasons why I don't taste a tequila and think to myself, *Oh! Paris!* There's a connection between what I taste and the identity, the historical and cultural significance, of the people who make it: an intrinsic relationship that I think of as *cultural terroir*. I wanted to understand more than just the soil composition and elevation of the agave fields from which my tequila came. More significant to me than the question of *what* something is made of, I realized, is the question of *why* it is made at all. Why do these spirits exist? How did they come to be? What history are they a part of, and why do we drink them today? These are the questions I tried to begin answering in this book.

From a crassly commercial point of view, spirits from Latin America are certainly "having a moment" here in the United States. If you look around, just about every celebrity these days seems to have a tequila brand. A decade or so ago, the rise in popularity of tequila in particular sparked a worldwide fascination with tequila's smokier cousin, mezcal (more on that in chapter one), and from there the list goes on and on. There's also a significant amount of interest in all things *artisanal* today. We want to get back to the essence of the thing, an essence that, in the world of food and beverage, lies in its human importance to the people who make it. Unlike, say, a lot of American bourbons, English gins, or Russian vodkas, many of the spirits of Latin America were, up until very recently, made on a small, preindustrialized scale. While this is changing—in some places dangerously quickly—many of the Latin spirits I love most are still made in a truly artisanal way.

My notion of cultural terroir finds a good parallel in the idea of *patria*. A concept also without a real equivalent in English—its translation from Spanish is something like "homeland," but it means so much more—*patria* is the embodiment not only of actual place but of that place's ethos and identity. It sums up one's national history, traditions, attitudes, and conception of belonging; it's what we feel pride and selfless devotion for when we are patriotic; and like patriotism, it has just as much to do with the intangible constructs of national selfhood as it does with physical borders.

We can't talk about the history of Latin America or the history of these spirits without talking about colonialism. During the centuries of colonization that began more than five hundred years ago, Europeans forced their customs on indigenous peoples across the Americas—changes that included new technologies such as distillation and the alembic still, and agricultural practices such as wine-grape cultivation. In many cases—and sometimes having no alternative but outright self-destruction—rather than rejecting these customs, the native people adapted them to their own ways, to survive while holding on to as much of their own traditions and histories as possible. Ancient gods continued to be venerated alongside new ones, ancient arts and rituals found a place among foreign ones, and food and drink, along with the many traditions surrounding them, underwent the same interweaving and transformation. New *patrias* arose, and the resulting racial mixture of European and indigenous blood and tradition is what we know as *mestizo* culture today.

In some parts of Latin America, especially the Caribbean islands, in support of the sugarcane industry that came to prominence there, another crucial factor was added to this cultural melting pot: the African slave trade. Out of the unique blending and mixture of the cultures of indigenous Americans, Europeans of various colonizing nations, and the West African slaves that the Europeans brought with them, again arose entirely new ethnic groups and traditional products, including the sugarcane spirit known as rum, which is still

Grapes, destined for singani production, being unloaded for pressing at Bodega Casa Real, Tarija, Bolivia.

one of the Caribbean's most notable exports. These groups and products are the cultural counterpart to the colonial intermixture that took place everywhere else in the region; and for this reason, though many people may not instinctively consider the Caribbean to be part of Latin America, it very much is.

Of course, to acknowledge and celebrate these entanglements of old and new, imported and endemic, is not to disregard that they came often as the result of genocide, slaughter, oppression, and the tragic rupture of the communities, families, and previously held identities of so many people. But human beings are incredibly resilient, and the human drive to make sense of and assert our reality can create beauty from the most devastating chaos. The spirits of Latin America are part of that appreciable beauty.

In this book, I've grouped these spirits into three families, according to their base materials: agave, sugarcane, and grape. But these groupings aren't just relevant in an ordinary terroir sense; they also represent different kinds of interaction between indigenous Americans and European colonizers. The agave plant, from which tequila and mezcal is made, is native to the Americas (and may have been distilled in Mexico even prior to the arrival of the Spanish). Grapes and grape spirits, by contrast, were a purely European import, and grape spirits of the Americas were developed in imitation of already-existing products back in Europe. Sugarcane spirits, that drinkable expression of *patria* as it arose in the various colonial territories where sugar was produced, represent the chaotic intermixture between indigenous and European traditions.

BASICS

In addition to understanding Latin spirits by the three families, we'll need to have a fundamental grasp of how the spirits themselves are made. In each section, I'll talk about this production process as it pertains to whatever family of spirits we're discussing and then provide recipes for some of my favorite cocktails made with those spirits. Before getting into the specifics of spirits-making in each chapter, it'll be useful to have a brief overview of the process in general, to carry with us as we go.

To start off with, we need a thing—something, anything—with sugar in it, or with starches in it that can be converted into sugar. Be it a grape, an agave, a sugarcane, or any other plant, the manner in which we grow it, nourish it in its growth, and ultimately collect its sugars will affect the final spirit. While I was in Cuba, Havana Club's *Maestro de Ron* (master of rum), Asbel Morales, told me, "A crooked tree will never grow straight," meaning that if the base material isn't good, no adulteration afterward can fix it. Knowing this, any good spirits producer will begin by giving a full life to the plant, granting it all of the nutrients it needs—with as few additional chemicals as possible—to become the best version of itself: the fullest, boldest little guy it can be.

Sometimes a little cooking has to happen after the harvest in order to transform the plant's starches into usable sugars that we can ferment. (For the purposes of this book, this pertains only to agaves.) Once this is done, we extract the plant's now-properly-sugary juices by squishing and squeezing and crunching the plant up in one manner or another, sometimes adding water to thin it out and get those sugar levels exactly where we want them. What we end up with are two things: debris from the plant, rid of its sugary content—called *bagasso* in Spanish, or *bagasse* in French and English—and the sweet juice that we'll use as the raw material of fermentation. In sugarcane production in particular, this juice is known as *guarapo* in Spanish and *jus* in French; but as it enters fermentation, it's more generally known as *must* in English, *mosto* in Spanish, and *vin* in French.

Fermentation is where the real magic of alcohol production happens, and in all of my travels, it's really where producers showed the most pride in their work. It's not just where the alcoholic kick comes from; it's also where the esters—the sweet- and fruity-smelling flavor compounds brought out in any given spirit—are also first formed, which many a booze nerd can, and will, spend eons discussing. During a visit to Rhum J.M in beautiful Martinique, I met the distillery's master blender, Karine Lassalle, who'd come from a background in chemistry to pursue her love of all things distilled. During a discussion of flavor and aroma in distillates—in which she very kindly refrained from getting too technical for me—she summed things up perfectly: "All alcohol flavors ultimately come from fermentation. Distillation only expresses what fermentation produces."

Cleaning the leftover agave fibers (bagasso) out of a copper still at Tequila Siete Leguas, Atotonilco El Alto, Jalisco, Mexico.

Alcoholic fermentation requires a simple mixture of three ingredients: sugar, water, and yeast. Put simply, yeasts are miniscule little creatures that, under the right conditions (that's where the water comes in), gobble up sugar and expel it as alcohol and carbon dioxide. At the end of this stage, the yeasts die in the alcoholic environment they have produced—maxing out the beer- or wine-like substance they've created at between 6 to 13 percent alcohol by volume—and then the process is done.

Both manufactured and airborne yeasts can be used in fermentation. Airborne yeasts, many would argue, create a more nuanced and localized flavor profile, but manufactured distiller's yeast is far more efficient and easier for the producer to control. Fermentation can last anywhere from a day or so to well over a week, or even longer; you'll find producers of some very funky stuff out there who boast of a fermentation process that runs upward of thirty days. The types of fermentation vessel used will vary from one spirit to another; stainless steel is most commonly used today, but people use everything from clay pots to holes in the ground. (In Jalisco, Mexico, the heart of tequila country, I saw age-old river stone with holes burrowed in it for fermenting the local raicilla.) What we end up with after fermentation are two important by-products: ethanol, which gives the spirit its actual alcoholic strength, and esters, the molecular compounds that give it flavor. Generally speaking, the longer the fermentation, the more esters are produced, and the lower the alcohol (ethanol) content will be.

If we want our end product to be boozier than 13 percent, distillation likely is going to be needed. This is an old science, with evidence in different parts of the Middle East, Africa, and Asia dating back thousands of years. By the twelfth century AD, when the technology reached southern Italy via its Arab neighbors, the process was common, and a number of still types existed. Most important for our purposes is the copper alembic still, which arrived in Spain and Portugal via Moorish traders and was carried by those nations' colonists with them to their "New World."

Stills are generally made from copper, which is uniquely temperature-conductive and boosts many flavor compounds. Copper stills can be incredibly beautiful, precisely crafted apparatus, and the art of making them is an old and revered one. When I was at the Siete Leguas distillery in Jalisco, I met a father-and-son duo who were responsible for building and maintaining the copper alembics of just about every tequila producer in the area. The care they took in their work was inspiring. Truly a craft within a craft, they assured me it was something only a certain sensibility could master; no machine will ever be able to caress and maneuver the supple metal as effectively as the human hand.

Though copper is the most-often used material, stills, like fermentation vessels, can be made of just about anything: wood, tree trunks, clay pots, fifty-gallon barrels. In Haiti, I once saw a still made out of an old train car. Whatever the material, the function of the apparatus remains the same: heat everything and allow the brew to boil, let the alcohol (which boils more quickly than water) evaporate first; cool that vapor to re-condense it into alcohol, separate this out in various stages and strengths of alcohol and purity, and proportion these parts the way you want for a nice distilled spirit. This technology comes in two basic forms, of which every type of still is a variation: the pot still and the column still.

The oldest and simplest of these types is the pot still, which, in its most basic form, is just that: a pot. Steam rises from the boiling wine or "wash" within, hitting a tightly fitted cap on top; this cap is kept cold to condense the alcohol-rich vapor, turning it back into liquid to make a spirit. No matter how the pot is heated, different chemical compounds evaporate and condense at different temperatures, and you definitely don't want all of them in your spirit. Some of them just taste bad; others are downright poisonous and (among other things) are responsible for many a moonshiner going blind. Generally speaking, the stuff you don't want comes out at the beginning and at the end of the distillation process, while the good stuff comes out in the middle; these parts are called, respectively, the heads, tails, and hearts. The selection process whereby the distiller separates out good from bad is called the cut.

Pot distillation, however, is not terribly efficient; with it, we usually have to distill a spirit multiple times to get it up to the proof we want. Getting a spirit up to 55 percent alcohol, for instance, just isn't possible with one pass through a pot still, and running it through multiple pot-distillations requires a lot of work.

Enter the column still. The typical column still used today is not much different from the original Coffey or "patent" still, as the device was named in 1830 by one of its early patent-holders, Irishman Aeneas Coffey. Also called the continuous still because of its, well, continuous process, a column still is composed of one or more giant metal columns with perforated cooling plates positioned inside at various heights. Heat is applied to the bottom of the still, and as the wash drips in, it evaporates, causing steam to rise up and condense at different levels. The more columns you use, the more "refined"—and neutral—the spirit will be. With this type of still, there is no need to clean, reheat, and redistill; it all happens in one uninterrupted flow. Figure out which plate height gives you the best result—that is, your hearts— and you can keep everything in the column, condensing and re-evaporating, until it reaches the alcohol by volume (ABV) you want, up to 95 percent alcohol. Now that's efficiency!

For some, the train stops after distillation: it's booze, after all, and it's ready to intoxicate. In much of Latin America, this raw, clear distillate would simply be called *aguardiente*—a generic name, something like our "firewater." (Though having had delicious aguardientes from all over Latin America, I can tell you: it can be *so* much more than fire!) *Aguardiente* is a term I will use throughout this book, and it has different specific meanings in different places. In Mexico it's what they might call tequila or mezcal that wasn't made according to the specific rules set out by Mexican law; in Cuba it's what they call sugarcane distillate before it's been blended and aged; in Peru it's what they call pisco made in Chile. At its most basic, however, *aguardiente* is a catchall term that just means "distilled spirit," unaged more often than not.

I have to admit, I'm partial to unaged spirits. In my first trip to Oaxaca when I was nineteen, when I was first introduced to what would become a life-long love of mezcal, I was essentially told, "Look, chica. This is delicious right off the still. Why cover it up?" In my opinion, the less adaptation of the spirit from its original form—whether by means of colorants, sugar, or time spent in barrels—the better. But many, if not most, of the world's drinkers prefer aged spirits these days; and so many, if not most, of the world's producers tend to age theirs.

This isn't universal in Latin spirits by any means. One big reason: aging is expensive. First you have to buy barrels. In most cases, these barrels are bourbon barrels from the United States. (This is true around the world, and not just with Latin spirits.) Why? Because bourbon barrels, by law, can be used only once in making American whiskey, so there are a lot of leftovers to go around— and they're close by! Then you have to let the spirit sit around in a warehouse

Aging rhum in French oak, Martinique.

(which costs money), be checked by employees (who cost more money), while it evaporates through the wood (which costs the most money)! The alcohol lost to evaporation, known as the angel's share (or devil's share, as one tequila producer joked while we walked around his musty barrel house), accounts for the loss of quite a lot of product every year: in the hotter climates of Latin America, it can range anywhere from 2 percent to as much as 15 percent per year. That's a whole lot of booze just disappearing into thin air.

Aging can be done using a number of different methods, most of which are intended to leave the spirit in contact with mellowing, flavor-and-color-imparting wood. The simplest way to do this is one barrel at a time, with larger or smaller barrels being used to impart different levels of woodiness to the spirit. The methods used, and whether or not they're a legislated part of the spirits-making process, vary from one place to another. I learned about this from Thibaut Hontanx, director of production at Rhum Clément, when I toured their impressive facilities on what I felt was a sweltering-hot day—but which was pretty standard for tropical Martinique. "For me, age statements mean nothing, because alcohol doesn't age at the same speed in different places," he told me. "Here, we have an angel's share of 8 percent per year. In Europe, it's 2; in Scotland maybe 1 . . . it's all different. An aged spirit's quality has more to do with the workmanship that goes into it, than the age statement itself."

Despite the fact that it can be over-simplistic (and just plain wrong) to think of older spirits as better, it's certainly a trend in the spirits world today. Blame it on Scotch, or maybe on cognac. There's a sense of righteousness that comes along with the desire to age spirits nowadays, and it's almost entirely misplaced. I like to think of aging as a wood frame encasing a painting or photo—a metaphor I adopted from Carlos Camarena, master distiller of El Tesoro and other excellent tequilas. The purpose of the frame is not to overtake the picture it's framing; it's there to enhance it and to give it a little emphasis. If the picture is ugly, wrapping it in a big, beautiful wood frame won't help; if the picture is beautiful, you wouldn't want to hide it that way either. Aging is the same: it's done well only if it lets us taste that raw material, that terroir of nature and humanity that's gone into making the spirit what it is.

GETTING BIG WITHOUT GETTING BAD

As Latin-spirits industries expand, it's tempting to make the generalization that big is bad. It's very difficult to maintain authenticity while maximizing productivity and profit, and a lot of the larger producers out there have certainly opted for quantity over quality. On the flip side, it's also easy to romanticize the poverty associated with small towns and small scales of production and to look askance at any efforts to bring small producers into the big-business fold.

There are definitely larger producers who are doing the right thing, just as there are smaller producers who aren't. Good large producers employ people and bring business to a lot of small farmers and distillers. This allows these people to keep doing what they've been doing for generations while enjoying the benefits and opportunities that international commerce brings. These benefits—from improved working conditions to college education for the kids—are absolutely good things, and romanticizing the lack of them is one way that bad producers avoid paying their workers what they deserve.

Del Maguey's Vida mezcal, for example, is in demand world-wide, but it is still made according to traditional practices and provides opportunities to the Oaxacan community. "I love that our producer's son can realistically think about what he wants to be when he grows up," Del Maguey's Misty Kalkofen told me. "I also love that his brother helps in the [distillery]—but there's choice now, and that's a good thing." Additionally, Tosba, a new mezcal producer far from the bustle of Oaxaca City, is actively engaged in bringing much-needed jobs to the area; the same is true of Appleton Estates in central Jamaica, where the tourist economy that supports the rest of the country is absent. The owners of the singani producer Rujero were very conscious of their effect on the local community; while I was visiting, they told me that one hectare of grapevines can lift a whole Bolivian family out of extreme poverty, and their goal as a company is to provide such resources and jobs to their community.

Rogelio Martinez Cruz, *mezcalero* for Del Maguey Mezcal. Santa Maria Albarradas, Oaxaca, Mexico.

REGULATION

Last, one major aspect of the production of these spirits today is the legal regulations that are meant to protect and regulate them. In this book, we'll refer to that set of laws broadly as Denominations of Origin, or DOs. DOs essentially delineate territories within which a given product must be made—territories thought to be essential to that product's origins and qualities, whether geographical or cultural—and often specify rules according to which it must be made in order to legally be called by that product's name. With DO protection comes important questions regarding the nature of property rights and cultural definition, both locally and transnationally. It can be a double-edged sword, with both benefits and detriments—and money to be gained and lost—on both sides of any given question. In their most negative aspects, DOs restrict a spirit's definition and identity by limiting it to spurious borders and definitions, robbing other traditional places and producers of the ability to call their spirit by a name that may bring it more economic or cultural value, and allowing for the monopolization of spirits markets both at home and abroad. (Oftentimes, even for small producers within a designated geographical location, the cost of DO certification can be prohibitively expensive.) The opposite side of this coin, however, is that DOs can also serve a very important purpose in preserving local heritage and protecting traditional products from adulteration by outside forces seeking to profit from what amounts to cultural appropriation.

    This is a crucial part of the discussion around Latin spirits today, because, unlike products such as whiskey or vodka whose international commercial boundaries have had a long time to establish themselves, a lot of Latin spirits are only just now being discovered by the rest of the world and, as a result, are only just now being widely commercialized and regulated. Because of this, corporate greed is infringing upon the practices behind these spirits, wielding financial and governmental power to regulate away many of the "inefficiencies" of traditional production that have given them such distinctive flavors and vital cultural terroir. In short, the cultures behind Latin spirits, along with the plants and methodologies used to make them, are currently in real danger, whether DOs exist for them or not. And protecting these cultures, plants, and methodologies from exploitation and extinction now requires the conscientious participation of consumers such as you and me, in purchasing and drinking Latin spirits in an ethically responsible way.

Globalism is really nothing new: it's been going on since human beings could walk across plains and sail across seas. But we are at a place in the history of our global society where our need for a better understanding of each other has become painfully obvious. We lack cultural solidarity, mutual appreciation, and—in a word—togetherness. Spirits may seem like a strange way to get at that, but they're not; as shareable cultural expressions and commercial products, fundamental to all human cultures, they're something we can truly share and appreciate about each other. They give us a way to think of ourselves as human beings, not just as individuals—they're a way to think about our *patrias*, where we come from and the traditions that make us who we are. Via these spirits, and these cocktails, we can gain a more real, more human awareness of one another.

AGAVE

Above: A blue agave envelops a cactus in Arandas, Jalisco, Mexico. **Page 20:** *Jimador* Guillermo Padilla shaves the sharp *pencas* off an agave for harvest. La Alteña, Arandas, Jalisco, Mexico.

The agave—a succulent, commonly mistaken for a cactus but in fact a closer relative to asparagus—is a plant totally different from just about everything else humans harvest. And unlike sugar and grapes, it was not brought to the Americas by European invaders, but was found there upon the Europeans' arrival, sprinkled in many varieties up and down the Sierra Madre. This fact—that the agave is *from* Latin America, rather than transplanted there— is represented in the uniqueness and diversity of agave spirits, and of the cultures surrounding them.

Agave distillates—specifically mezcal and tequila—are the best starting place for *the* experience of Latin American spirits. Within this vibrant, diverse family of spirits, agave distillates are arguably the most objectively "New World": in flavor and feeling, no other spirit is quite like them.

Agaves were harvested in Mexico long before mezcal or tequila ever existed, and they have been used for many purposes by Mexican peoples over thousands of years. Many legends about the agave (or *maguey*, as it is called in Mexico) exist in indigenous Mexican folklore expressing how exceptionally useful—yet exceptionally defiant—the plant is.

And defiant is exactly what agaves are. They're Jurassic plants in appearance: hard, spiny, and harsh. They flourish in equally dramatic and variant range of terrain. Within Oaxaca alone, I drove through parched switchbacks in the cactus-spiked desert mountains of Candelaria de Yegolé in the south, all the way up to steep jungle canyons full of mist and lush, dark-green tropical foliage surrounding the Rio Cajonos in the north. In the south, fine sand coats every layer of clothing, and everything feels rocky and arid; in the north, the humidity is such that a bathing suit may never fully dry. In all of these diverse environments, agaves can be found growing strong.

The plant's name bears the stamp of impressiveness in its Greek root-word, *agauos*, which means "noble"—venerable, mature, and proud. Agaves don't grow in a season; rather they take many, many years—anywhere from five to upward of thirty!—to fully mature. The *pencas,* the leaflike blades that surround the plant, are needle-sharp at the ends, with razor-like *dentes,* or teeth, fanning out along the edges to defend the plant from its predators. Once the agave is harvested—a battle in itself—it takes many days to cook and sometimes weeks to ferment. I can't imagine the first person who saw one of these barbed plants and got the idea of trying to get to the middle of it somehow, much less subjecting it to the battery of operations required to get an alcoholic beverage out of it.

Whoever that person was, it is generally agreed that he or she was an Aztec. The agave and pulque (the fermented beer-like beverage made from its nectar) were so central to Aztec culture that an image of the plant was used to represent the Aztec goddess of fertility and life, Mayahuel. The technique of cooking the agave and fermenting its juices to obtain pulque was known in Mexico as early as 6500 BC, and beverages made from the maguey were used in many social rites, from everyday homeopathic traditions, some of which persist today, to intense religious ceremonies in which its intoxicating properties muted the pain of self-cutting and autosacrifice. (This is reflected in the medicinal purposes for which agave distillates are used in more recent history as well: as an ointment for cuts or stings, as a cure-all for illness, as a magical remedy. There's a rural Mexican tradition that still survives, of spitting mezcal over a person to rid them of fear or pain. I saw it done on a farm in Oaxaca where our hostess had just suffered a dog bite.)

Among the Aztecs and other indigenous Mexican peoples, the agave plant was, and still is, used in many ways beyond the inebriating ones with which we are most familiar today. The *pencas* can be used whole to shingle houses or fuel fires. The *quiotes* (the asparagus-like flowering pistil of the plant, which can grow to an impressive twenty feet or more in height), when dried, make sturdy fence posts and house beams; fresh *quiotes* are also ground up with corn and made into tortillas. Fibers from the *pencas* are collected to make threads for textiles, bags, carpets, and fishing equipment. The sharp *dentes* from the leaves have been used as pins and nails, or (keeping a single long fiber attached) as a convenient needle and thread. Even the plant's stubby white roots are used to make brooms or coarse fibers for weaving. The cooked *piña*, or heart, of the agave can be eaten like an artichoke, used to make soap, or (in the case of certain species) applied as a treatment for snakebites. As seventeenth-century Spanish priest Francisco Ximenez summarized so well, "The plant alone would be sufficient to provide all things necessary for human life." No wonder it was regarded as a goddess!

It is in the fine spirits distilled from the agave that we find the most enduring and condensed example of this mestizo cultural amalgamation, a little silver lining to the devastation wrought by the Spanish (and other

Harvested blue agave hearts waiting to be cooked in brick ovens at Tequila Cascahuín, El Arenal, Jalisco, Mexico.

Fernando Rangel takes a break while unloading agaves at the distillery. Tequila Cascahuín, El Arenal, Jalisco, Mexico.

European forces') colonization of the Americas. The native people had a deep history of love for the intoxicating pulque that came from the plant, and increasing evidence from many sources suggests that they distilled spirits from it, too, perhaps hundreds of years before the Spanish arrived. But nonetheless, the Spanish did bring techniques of distillation with them, often using these techniques to subdue the native populations as they conquered them. New spirits arose as a physical embodiment of the mix of cultures that was forcibly produced there, the spirits around which much of Mexican culture revolves today: mezcal, its offshoot tequila, and others.

Many of these spirits have become known outside of Mexico only in the last few decades; and in those few decades, all agave spirits have experienced a continuous rise in popularity worldwide, a popularity that other Latin spirits are aiming to emulate. Along with this boom, predictably, has come serious controversy, as the network of traditions and practices that underpin the maguey and its many uses comes into contact with a growing global agave-spirits industry.

The present-day discourse about agave distillates is full of arguments over where the spirits originated and under what circumstances; who makes them best and how; the right and wrong industrial, agricultural, and environmental practices for their production; and on and on. And the passion behind these arguments makes perfect sense, when you recognize that, more so than any of the other spirits we will talk about in this book, these spirits began, and continue to function, as intrinsic elements of their native country's culture, as anciently and inextricably linked to every aspect of Mexican life as the maguey itself. "Right now, we know agave distillates in Mexico as the result of the mix of cultures," says Pedro Jimenez Guirria of Mezonte in Guadalajara, one of the greatest minds in agave spirits today. "But the fact that the plant was *always* considered sacred in Mexico, and still is, has given the agave-spirits category a special place in the history of Mexico and its people." This integration is seen everywhere in Mexico: from the appearance of the agave and its products in artistic and cultural traditions large and small to the familial teams of brothers and sisters, parents and children who often work the fields and distilleries together. Simply put, agave spirits grew up in step with Mexican culture, both before and after the arrival of the Spanish; and any treatment of them in isolation from that culture—industrial, academic, or otherwise—violates the spirits and the culture together.

PRE-HISPANIC MEXICAN DISTILLATION

The usual account of the introduction of distillation into Mexico by the Spanish is only the best-documented one. Strong arguments make the case for the existence of pre-Hispanic distillation; and in my recent travels in Mexico, the debate over this topic was one of the biggest controversies I found raging around the country's native distillates, among master *mezcaleros* and local scholars alike.

Through archeological digs and related studies, scientists have discovered pottery and burnt-soil fragments with traces of agave that they say provide evidence of distillation going back many centuries BC. A broad variety of stills continue to be used in Mexico today—many more than simply the alembic stills that the Spanish brought with them—and many of the most traditional types closely echo early stilling technology found elsewhere in the world: specifically, the characteristic cooking utensils of the Far East, originated during the Shang and Zhou periods of 1600 to 221 BC. Again, scholars have pointed to archaeological evidence for these stills' use on the west coast of Mesoamerica hundreds of years before the arrival of the Spanish.

There are very often two sides to the pre-Hispanic-distillation coin, and strong arguments being made on both. But the evidence for pre-Hispanic distillation is already compelling, and only stands to grow as academic interest in the subject increases. Siembra Spirits' David Suro, one of the industry's most passionate voices on the subject, told me, "We have not dedicated enough time to our genesis as a culture of agave spirits. I truly believe that in five to ten years, everyone will agree that distillation started pre-Hispanically. We're just waiting for more information to come forward."

Before we get into the modern history and production of this quintessential Latin spirit, a quick note on terminology.

When it comes to agave distillates, most people in America (and many other places outside of Mexico) know of tequila long before they know of mezcal. Tequila is undoubtedly more popular worldwide; it has more celebrity-owned and star-studded brands, more rappers singing about it, more college students and resort-goers shooting it. Mezcal, by contrast, is not only lesser known but it is also "stronger" in flavor to many palates; it strikes many unaccustomed drinkers as having the same relation to tequila that, say, a very peaty single-malt Scotch whisky might have to bourbon. Consequently, people in America tend to think of mezcal as an offshoot of tequila, but in fact, it's the other way around. In reality, we cannot have tequila without mezcal, and it makes sense for us to start—as I happened to have done accidentally in my own experience with Latin spirits—with mezcal.

For hundreds of years, the word *mezcal* has been used generally, to describe any and all spirits made from the cooked heart of the agave. The word comes from two indigenous Nahuatl words, *metl* (referring to agave or maguey) and *ixcalli* (from *ixca*, meaning to bake or cook, and *-tli*, a noun suffix). Historically, anything—anything at all—distilled from the fermented liquid of a cooked agave was called mezcal, in this general sense. (The Spanish, early in their Mexican distillation experience, referred to pulque as *vino de mezcal* for this reason.) Just about every part of Mexico had its own history and process of mezcal production, representative of the local climate, land, native agaves, and (most important) cultural background. Tequila—one type of agave spirit distilled in one particular region of Mexico from one particular kind of agave— was originally a mezcal in this sense: all squares are four-sided shapes, all cognac is brandy, and all tequila, bacanora, raicilla, et cetera, are mezcal.

Well . . . kinda.

The confusion began in 1994, when—hoping to repeat the success that tequila had enjoyed abroad—the Mexican government decided to grant mezcal its own Denomination of Origin (DO). This legislation limited the states that could be legally recognized as producers of mezcal, laid down a set of parameters for making the spirit, and created a regulatory body, the Consejo Regulador del Mezcal (CRM), to ensure compliance with them. As with any legal restriction, this legally limited the meaning of the word *mezcal* to a very

A fieldworker uses a spade and mallet to chop through the tough roots of an agave. San Baltazar Chichicapam, Oaxaca, Mexico.

spccific family of spirits, which has since led to a lot of complications. (We'll get into that later.)

As double-edged as the 1994 ruling was, it is nonetheless legally defini-tive; and so, for the purposes of this book, when I use the word *mezcal*, I will be using the term in its specific sense to mean an agave spirit coming from one of the recognized states listed in mezcal's Denomination of Origin. When I mean "mezcal" in the general sense—as any spirit distilled from the fermented liquid of a cooked agave—I'll use the terms *agave distillate* or *agave spirit.*

HISTORY

Recorded evidence of the consumption of agave spirits in Mexico goes back almost to the earliest days of the Spanish occupation in the sixteenth century (and, I believe, much earlier). It is spectacular that these spirits and their traditions have managed to survive over so many centuries; they've certainly had to contend with plenty of opposition. In 1641, in the early days of the Spanish colonization efforts, the Spanish Crown enacted a tax (effectively amounting to a ban) on their new territories' wine exports, in an effort to prevent the competition from harming Spanish producers back at home. This encouraged the production and exportation of distilled spirits all over Latin America, however it also resulted in a whole set of powerful, long-lasting social stigmas being attached to the new spirits both at home and abroad. In contrast to the "civilized" beverages still being imported from Europe for those who could afford them—cognac, Scotch, and so forth—the new agave spirits were dismissed as cheap firewater, the stuff of the uneducated and unworthy, and the reputation stuck. Long afterward—even into present times—agave spirits have been widely associated with a cheap yellow bottle, with or without a worm in it; this stigma held on well into the 1990s, when these distillates began to be popularly recognized for the fine, delicious distillates they are.

But the spirits and the traditions that sprang up around them in Mexico endured nonetheless. In the early years of the wider popularization of agave spirits in the eighteenth century, the spirits were embraced by many as part of a unique Mexican national identity. Rather than imbibing the old European spirits that the hoity-toity set was drinking, a large portion of the country's working population began to embrace agave spirits as their own, incorporating them first into the idea of Mexico as its own cultural entity, then, after the country gained independence throughout the turbulent nineteenth century, into its identity as a nation.

The California gold rush of the mid-nineteenth century, largely fueled by the tequila of its south, first cemented the worldwide demand for agave spirits. Despite still being seen most often as a lower-class beverage, tequila was soon universal. When the Mexican Revolution came along to finally solidify Mexican independence in the early twentieth century, tequila became synonymous with Mexico. As Tomas Estes emphasizes in his book, *The Tequila Ambassador*, the importance of the spirit in this context cannot be overstated: the period "was part of an emotionally, spiritually charged Mexican epoch, as different mixes of Indian and European blood fought each other and helped define what their existence and identity was all about. . . . The destiny of this nation of people was being shaped and inspired by what was fast becoming their national drink. For those fighting for a new life, tequila was the perfect fuel. Tequila would warm, give courage, take away pain and stimulate dreams."

Just as the Mexican Revolution was coming to an end, another event of enormous significance for worldwide spirits consumption was beginning: American Prohibition. Mexico, being the closest neighbors to the south, experienced an immediate explosion of alcohol tourism, particularly in Tijuana and other easily accessible border towns. Tequila's popularity soared as Americans began to make trips over, even for just one day at a time, to wet their palates with the "Mexican whiskey."

The 1950s and 1960s then saw tequila become more popular worldwide, and despite the blemish of baseness that still hung over the spirit, tequila producers began to grow larger and larger, giving rise to a new phenomenon: the global tequila industry. With powerful conglomerates investing millions in the spirit, more and more legal regulations arose to control its creation and earn money on its taxes, beginning with tequila's official Denomination of Origin in 1977, the first DO to be recognized outside of Europe.

Tequila quickly became *the* Latin spirit abroad—the best-known spirit south of the border in the United States and elsewhere. Today Americans drink it at an ever-increasing rate: in shots and cocktails, from cheap flasks to expensive collectible bottles. Readily adopted into pop culture by rappers and country musicians alike, it has made movie stars even richer than before as the hobby of tequila-making has taken hold in Hollywood. And in America as everywhere else, it's known as the hard-party booze *par excellence*, as generation after generation of people young and old follow the mantra of "One tequila, two tequila, three tequila, floor" to delight and disaster.

Mezcal's global popularization came later, and more painfully. Up until the 1970s, the spirit was produced all over Mexico, almost exclusively in small, family-run distillery houses, or *palenques* or *fabricas*, each of which was connected to a number of neighboring communities. People would buy mezcal from their local *mezcalero* whenever they needed it for one collective purpose or another— generally festivals, parties, religious ceremonies, and so on. Then around this time, a few shady people within Mexico had an idea: why not make a great big amount of some cheaper, crappier spirit; slap the name "mezcal" on the bottle; and sell it at a lower price? Nobody had yet taken the time to specify what mezcal really was, so the shady producers figured that all the locals would care about was getting more bang for their buck.

They were right. As Asis Cortés of El Jolgorio and Casa Cortés told me, during those years, the nearly four hundred small producers in operation in Oaxaca's Santiago Matatlán, the "World Capital of Mezcal," were priced out of business and narrowed down to just forty, and cheap knockoff "mezcal" dominated the market at home and abroad. Following Cortés around to a handful of surviving distilleries and farms in Santiago Matatlán, I saw some of the results of this narrowing-down, from the tiny and often down-to-the-dirt-basic traditional distilleries remaining to the shockingly large mezcal factories that arose to take their places.

It was partly in response to this rampant unscrupulousness—though more out of a desire to capitalize on mezcal's rising commercial viability, à la tequila—that mezcal was granted its own DO in 1994. This led to a tightening-down on the mezcal being produced, which helped open the door for better mezcal producers to evangelize their product abroad.

The early 2000s brought an unpredicted interchange between traditional *mezcaleros* and foreign chefs and sommeliers, who recognized in mezcal a high-quality spirit worth paying for. A decade later, Oaxaca started to become a tourist destination; a few years after that, proper mezcal prices began to be accepted locally as more and more Mexican drinkers embraced their native spirit.

Today, tequila and mezcal represent industries of prodigious size within Mexico. Both *tequileros* and *mezcaleros* large and small produce their spirits in conformity with a vast, constantly changing set of rules and regulations—rules as often cursed for the limitations they place on the spirits' production as they are lauded for the protections they grant. These legal issues loom very large in the world of agave spirits today, and I will discuss them in greater detail later. For now, let's get into the process by which these unique spirits are produced.

PRODUCTION

Venture out into the more rural areas where agave spirits are produced today, and you'll find that the situation is still not too far from the romanticized image of a weathered man (or usually a man) going out into the hills with a donkey, harvesting a couple of wild agaves and bringing them back home to cook, grind up, ferment, and distill. In contrast to the well-established agricultural communities of the Tequila Valley, mezcal country is largely rural, and often small-scale in feel; I never know quite what to expect there. Contrary to the idea many outsiders have of a uniformly dusty, dry Mexico, the country's environments are incredibly diverse, encompassing everything from deserts to jungles, ocean cliffs to dense forests, and high mountain ranges to lush beaches. Even the drier climates where agaves typically flourish are often vibrant with the colors emulated in Mexican art and culture: mineral rocks of bright green, yellow, and purple; rich black volcanic soils; and clay bright red with iron oxide. And the agaves found in such places, often growing wild are similarly diverse.

With tequila, though multiple varietals of agave were once commonly used, only one type is now legally allowed: the highly efficient *tequilana* Weber, aka the Blue Weber agave or blue agave as it is commonly called. Visit the farmlands of Jalisco, and you can't miss the endless rows of this intensively cultivated plant stretching over hills and valleys; even from a distance, as you drive in along the roads from the mountains of Arandas to the Tequila Valley, you'll see its beautiful blue color tinging the hillsides. With mezcal, on the other hand, at least fifty different types of agave are used—from long, sword-like Espadins or Karwinskis with stalks like tree trunks topped with bristling fronds to squat-leafed, water lily–esque Cupreata or giant Tepeztate with broad, tonguelike pencas twisting chaotically in every direction. Many of these plants are found growing in incredibly tricky-to-reach places—cliffsides or steep ravines, for example, where trucks can't drive—and must be har-vested carefully and transported by hand or pack animal back to the *palenque* or *fabrica,* or distillery, where they will be made into a spirit.

Agaves belong to the Agavaceae family, which is native to the Americas. The plants span almost the entire length of the continent, being found every-where from Canada and the United States to Bolivia and Paraguay. More than two hundred species of Agavaceae exist, of which nearly 80 percent are native to Mexico. The states within Mexico with the widest variety of agaves are Oaxaca, Chihuahua, Sonora, Coahuila, Durango, and Jalisco, but (for some reason) only two of these, Oaxaca and Durango, are specified within the thir-teen current DO-recognized mezcal-producing states. Among the wide variety of agaves used in mezcal production, the most popular species is the *Agave angustifolia.* This species spans the largest geographical and ecological area of all agaves, being found from Sonora to Chiapas; and if we're going by the scientific classification, many, many agaves—including Espadin, the type most commonly used in mezcal—go under its guise.

Both tequila and mezcal have limited regions in Mexico in which they can be legally produced. At the time of this writing, the total list of approved mezcal-producing states includes Oaxaca, Durango, Guanajuato, Guerrero, San Luis Potosí, Tamaulipas, Zacatecas, Michoacán, Puebla, Estado de Mexico, and Aguascalientes. Tequila must be produced in one of five states: Guanajuato, Michoacán, Nayarit, Tamaulipas, and (most famously) Jalisco.

In the wild, agaves are pollinated by insects, birds, and (most often) bats, the latter of which are dusted with the plants' pollen when they swoop in to drink nectar from the agave flowers, which open at night. However, many agaves also have the unique property of reproducing asexually by a natural pro-cess of subdivision, whereby the mother plant shoots off little clones of itself. Cutting one of these clones—called a *hijuelo*—and replanting it is the simplest

Cecilio Fabian washes out a pot still at the *palenque* of Rey Campero. Candelaria de Yegolé, Oaxaca, Mexico.

way for a farmer to grow a new agave. This type of agave propagation also makes a lot of sense from a spirits-making point of view. When agaves flower and reproduce sexually, as they tend to do when left to their own devices, the parent plant grows a long treelike *quiote*, which draws all of its sugars away from the heart of the plant. This ultimately renders the rest of the plant worthless for liquor production, so propagating the plant by *hijuelos* instead, and interrupting the plant's sexual process by cutting off the *quiote* before it fully grows, is what most producers opt to do.

THE MYSTERY MIXTO

While it's true that tequila has to be made from blue agave, that's really only half the story—or rather, a little more than half. In the early days of Big Tequila, as some *tequileros* still recall, all tequila was made entirely from blue agave. Then, feeling the pinch of one agave shortage or another, some tequila producers agitated for the laws to be changed, to allow a small percentage of other material to be introduced into the mix. Once that door was thrown open, each subsequent agave shortage brought new requests for the bar to be lowered even further.

Now, in order to be legally called tequila, the agave spirit in question only has to be a measly 51 percent blue agave. The other 49 percent can be quite literally anything you want. (Ironically, tequila's DO, which is supposed to protect the spirit as a national product, prevents the use of other agaves in mixtos, while allowing their producers to incorporate all sorts of mind-bogglingly nontraditional ingredients, such as U.S.-made corn syrup.) Quite a lot of so-called tequilas out there are these mystery mixes. It's no wonder that college students the world over get sick from the stuff; they don't even know what's in it!

Now that I've mentioned these tequilas, I'm going to do what most people do after their first experience drinking one: never speak of them again. If it's tequila, it ought to be made from blue agave, and blue agave only.

Whether grown in the wild (in which case they're referred to by the name *silvestre*) or commercially cultivated on farms and estates, agaves represent a range of terroir matched by few other crops in the world. Generally, agaves are cultivated, whether that property is a series of broad expanses in the Tequila highlands or the sloping planes of Michocan's Tierra Caliente, and driving through much of Mexico, you can see rows and rows of the spiny plants. However, simply because an estate grows agaves does not mean it also distills agave spirits. As with vine growers and winemakers, those who grow the plants and those with the resources to make distillates from them are often two distinct groups, and many distillers end up buying agaves grown elsewhere to make their spirits. Obviously, this can seriously muddy the waters when we talk about terroir. It also makes the agave market, especially the notoriously nasty one in Jalisco, have agave prices—frequently dictated by massive companies without much regard for either agave farmers or smaller producers elsewhere—prone to dramatic rises and falls.

This kind of complexity in flavor profile is a very good reason why it's not sensible to expect "consistency" (in terms of sameness) among these spirits. As consumers, we've been conditioned to expect consistency in a lot of the food and drink we consume—a McDonald's hamburger is designed to taste the same wherever in the world you buy it, as are many of the commercial spirits made by big brands. But it's not sensible to expect this kind of consistency among agave spirits, or any truly artisanal product. Agaves' complex flavor, extremely long growth period, and year-round harvest makes them arguably even less predictable than, say, wine grapes, which are never expected to be the same from year to year; throw in the unpredictability that fermentation and distillation introduce into the equation, and consistency starts to look like a pretty silly ask. La Alteña's Carlos Camarena said it well when he joked, "The only constant with us is variability."

In agave spirits and other spirits—as well as with many, many other things—we should learn to look for a different kind of consistency: consistency of quality. The best agave-spirits producers know this well and embrace the traditional qualities that make their spirit a little messier than others; in a good way.

TERROIR WITH AGAVE

About ten years ago, it was generally assumed that distillation removed any notion of terroir. But now—thanks largely to efforts by enthusiastic agave-spirits producers such as David Suro and Tomas Estes—that's changing. And no family of spirits makes a better argument for terroir than agave spirits, whose base materials grow year-round in a broad variety of tastable, feelable conditions.

Consider the wide divergence in terroir between highland and valley tequila. The agaves of the valley produce a spirit of a brighter, more peppery-herbaceous character; it literally tastes greener. (I actually prefer aged tequilas from here, like the Fortaleza Añejo, because the boldness of valley-grown agave can bite through otherwise overpowering oak notes.) By contrast, when I visit La Alteña's farms in the highlands, I find cooler conditions and red-clay soil that (I was told) contains higher levels of iron and potassium. Agaves grown here tend to have both a higher sugar content and higher levels of minerality and acidity, and this results in tequilas that are lighter and more intricate, brinier, and more floral.

For harvesting the mature agave, the process differs geographically, as do the words used for it. With mezcal in Oaxaca, for instance, it's usually called the *cortar*, or "cutting." In tequila-making Jalisco, it's called the *jima*, from the Nahuatl word *xima*, "to shear." (Interestingly, the Nahua people also used this word metaphorically to mean "die," since it was thought that the spirits of the dead were shorn of their hair to become slaves in the next world.) As always with crops destined for the distillery, the goal is to harvest the agaves once they've reached optimal ripeness, when they're bursting with sugar.

Then comes the battle. The harvester's real art is the wielding of a razor-sharp blade—either a long-bladed machete or a round spadelike *coa* popularly used in Jalisco—to harvest the *piñas*, or heart of the agave. It's a craft that has been passed down through generations, and to this day, no machine can do it better. Slicing through the *pencas* and roots, the harvester frees the *piñas*, where all of the plants' sugars are concentrated. In this process, the harvester shears the *pencas* down to a particular closeness, depending on the type of agave being harvested and the end flavor desired. Generally speaking, since the *pencas* constitute the fibrous, bitter part of the plant, the closer they're cut, the sweeter (and, as some point out, potentially less complex in flavor) the product will be.

Whether cultivated or grown in the wild, agaves are extremely hardy plants and generally demand very little attention or care while they grow. The *piñas* of mature agaves range in size from about the size of a volleyball, on the smaller end, up to that of a large wine barrel.

THE COST OF AGAVES

Agave prices are increasing at unprecedented rates, in some cases reaching highs of 27 pesos (about $1.50) per kilo. The big question is, if this is the case, and we also know how labor-intensive agave spirits can be to make, why are tequilas and mezcales in today's market still being made available at prices that don't even cover the cost of the raw material used to make them? At a cost of 27 pesos per kilo of agave hearts, a liter of tequila would require nearly $9 worth of agaves alone—not including associated costs such as labor, packaging, shipping, or taxes!

Few tequilas are priced to reflect these costs, so someone's getting the short end of the stick. I can tell you it isn't the big brands; it's the *jimadores* and *cortadores* in the fields. Especially because the agave-spirits industry is still relatively new and most of the smaller farmers working for it are unused to the cutthroat practices of big business, the farmers are open to exploitation. And many of the big brands use their leverage to force small farmers to commit to certain yields and prices ahead of time, so that when prices fluctuate, it's the farmers who have to bear the brunt of it. Buy appropriately!

SUSTAINABILITY IN AGAVE SPIRITS

Though it's often referred to vaguely as "agave shortage," the problem of agave overharvest is no secret in Mexico. It's gotten so bad lately, in fact, that at the end of the twentieth century, some tequila producers took to illegally importing truckloads of agave hearts from other parts of the country. This is increasingly a problem with wild agaves, whose value is higher in some places; but agave spirits in general show no sign of lessening in popularity, so overharvest stands to be a pressing problem in years to come.

Overharvest is hardly the only threat facing the industry. Genetic mono-culture, resulting from hijuelo propagation, is potentially a much bigger one. Many of the blue agaves in Jalisco right now—95 percent of those grown for tequila—are the product of this type of breeding: they are essentially many, many clones of just a few plants. Though easy and cost-efficient for producers, it's a dream that could turn nightmarish very quickly: lack of biodiversity equals a more uniform structure of disease immunity, so one nasty strain of agave plague is all it would take to put every last one of these plants in danger.

Recognizing that growing from seed strengthens and adds variety to the plant, some producers have been allowing a percentage of their agaves to go to seed, in order to fortify the species as a whole. Other solutions are found in initiatives such as the Bat Friendly Project, spearheaded by Rodrigo Medellín and David Suro. The project centers around encourag-ing bats to pollinate agaves, allowing the plants to propagate sexually and thus diversify their genetic stock. To be certified Bat Friendly, a producer has to allow 5 percent of their agaves to go to seed, rendering them useless for spirits production—but providing genetic strength for generations to come.

Agave nurseries are another new approach to sustainability that some producers are taking. Graciela Angeles at Mezcal Real Minero is responsible for an agave-nursery project called Proyecto LAM, which works in cooperation with the distillery. "We reproduce every single agave we use by seed," she said, "and we continue even with agaves we don't make mezcal with, in order to preserve them for the future." Some producers are also replanting not only agaves but also the woods used as fuel to roast them and power the stills.

Agave seeds heading for the nursury, Real Minero, Santa Catarina Minas, Oaxaca, Mexico.

The agave harvest is *tough* work that the field workers take great pride in. In Arandas, Jalisco, while visiting La Alteña, I met three jimador brothers who worked the fields there together every day, selecting the agaves and cutting them down in blazing midday heat. While in Oaxaca, I went out on one particularly scorching day to chat with Faustino Garcia Vasquez, who makes, among other delicious things, Del Maguey's wonderful Chichicapa mezcal. Pausing now and then to shout in Zapotec to the other men in the fields, he told me of his family and their dedication to the agave, with *mezcaleros* and *cortadores* going back generations.

After the harvest, the conversion of the agave's bitter starches into sugars to allow for fermentation begins. This is done in a myriad of ways, depending on from where in Mexico the spirit in question hails, and who's doing the cooking: it can be done in earthen pits, in traditional brick ovens (called *hornos*), in autoclaves (essentially massive pressure cookers), or in diffusers. All methods are not created equal, however, and the ones I've just mentioned are (in my opinion) listed in order of best to worst in terms of their capacity to make a delicious spirit. It is, after all, a process of roasting that we're doing here, and as with your Thanksgiving turkey, a long, slow roast is best. You wouldn't wait until four in the afternoon on Thanksgiving Day to cut your turkey into little pieces and throw them in the microwave; would you? No. You'd wake up at four in the *morning* and slow-cook that bird until the meat was falling off the bones—and the same goes for cooking agaves.

With the notable exception of mezcal from San Luis Potosí—which, like many traditional tequilas, is made in a steam-heated *horno*—agaves destined for mezcal are generally cooked in underground stone pits, using different woods endemic to the area. This imparts a degree of smokiness to the finished product, the flavor for which mezcal is most widely known.

In any case, a properly cooked agave is a much more manageable object than an uncooked one. Shorn of its formidable spikes, chopped up, and cooked, it's textured a bit like a massive artichoke; it is this material that must then be pulverized to extract the agave's sweet juices, or *aguamiel*, from its tough fibers. This can be accomplished in a number of ways, within all of which the end goal is to reduce the cooked agaves' juices to a sweet, syrupy mash (the *mosto* or must), with the remaining fibers (*bagasso*) either integrated into that mash or discarded, again depending on style and place.

PECHUGA

Pechuga has long been revered in agave-spirits lore as one of the most special mezcales of all, reserved for occasions and fiestas. It's inherently a small-production spirit, made later in fall to early winter, mostly because in making it, the *mezcalero* takes valuable mezcal and runs it through another costly distillation, where the still is filled not only with booze but also with fruit, herbs, and nuts of the harvest season.

Oh, and meat.

Traditionally, pechuga's second or third distillation incorporates the breast of some kind of poultry (*pechuga* means "breast" in Spanish), which is hung within the still so that the vapors of the distillation pass over and through it before condensing. At the end, you're left with a new, ultraflavorful mezcal—and a leathery hard ball of petrified meat.

It gets weirder. I've had pechugas at Mezonte in Guadalajara that were made with snake meat and venison; Del Maguey has even created an extremely luxurious one that uses a whole Iberico ham. The possibilities are endless—and believe me, the results are worth the extra effort! Flavors vary with these interesting spirits, but never have I tasted one that tastes like a Christmas ham or a Thanksgiving turkey. Rather, they tend to be extremely fruit-forward, due to the fruits added to the distillation; depending on the type of meat used, they can also sometimes be quite gamey.

Luckily for us, many brands are now exporting their own marks of pechuga, though most of them feature poultry rather than the weird stuff. I particularly like Tosba's pechuga, as well as Del Maguey's.

COOKING METHODS

STONE/EARTHEN PIT Popularly used in a lot of mezcal production, this cooking method is what tends to give mezcal its characteristic smoky smell. A deep hole is dug into the earth and lined with stones. A slow-burning fire is then built inside it and allowed to burn, creating coals and heating the stones. Agave *piñas* are then layered in, covered with earth and *bagasso*, and cooked, typically for three to five or even thirty days or more.

HORNO OR BRICK OVEN Mostly perceived as a tequila-making technique, this method is actually popular in the production of other agave spirits as well. In this method, the agave *piñas* are packed into an aboveground oven of brick, stone, or clay and cooked with condensed steam for anywhere from a day and a half to four days.

AUTOCLAVE An agave autoclave is essentially a pressure cooker the size of an eighteen-wheel truck. It works just as a pressure cooker does: you seal everything in and then build up pressure with steam and heat to cook what's inside, fast. This can reduce the cooking time of an agave to as little as eight hours. Autoclaves are preferred by some—like Calle 23's Sophie Decobecq—for their exactitude, and for imparting no additional cooking flavors to the agave.

DIFFUSER Hailed by some as the most efficient tool for extracting sugars from agaves, the high-tech diffuser is generally looked down upon by the world's agave enthusiasts. In this process, raw agave is shredded into thumb-size pieces and then placed into the enclosed diffuser, where it is pressure-washed with hot water (and sometimes chemicals) to extract the plant's starches. This procedure does not cook the juice enough to fully convert the starches to sugar, so the juice and fibers are usually boiled before being fermented. Diffusers are controversial not only because they're antithetical to tradition—a diffuser does in two hours what it takes an horno days to accomplish—but also because they allow for the use of immature and improperly cut agaves, which has ramifications all along the agricultural line.

Workers at Real Minero remove agaves from the earthen oven after days of cooking. Santa Catarina Minas, Oaxaca, Mexico.

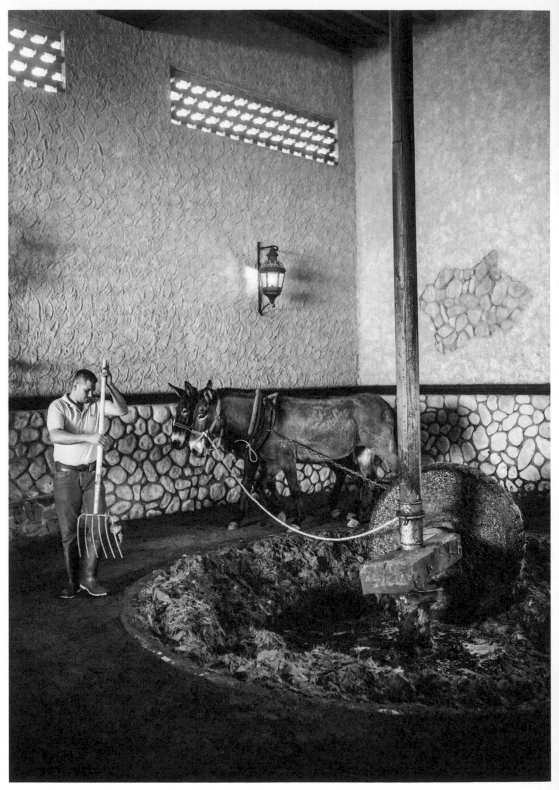

Mules crush oven-roasted agaves in a traditional *tahona*. Tequila Siete Leguas, Atotonilco El Alto, Jalisco, Mexico.

On the most traditional end of the spectrum, pulverizing agaves is accomplished either by hand, using (no kidding) large clubs and axes, or in a round pit mill, using an enormous wheel. This wheel—in tequila production it is called a *tahona*; in mezcal-making the whole pit-and-wheel combo is simply called a *molino*—is generally made out of either cut stone or cement. The stone is then attached to a pillar in the middle of the mill by a rotating arm, which allows the wheel to circle inward from the pit's edge. To use it, you toss your agave fibers into that pit; attach a horse, donkey, cow, or tractor (if you can afford it) to the wheel; and set the whole thing going in a dizzyingly small circle, continuously shoveling the stuff under the wheel until—voilà!—a few (or not so few) hours later, the fibers are thoroughly crushed and your horse, donkey, cow, or tractor driver is bored to tears. On my first trip to Oaxaca in 2005, I was blown away by this process: the smoke drifting in from the open oven nearby, the donkey circling and smashing the agaves with his driver walking wordlessly alongside him, the hypnotic silence hanging over the whole scene. Hypnotic is really what it is; it's very easy to lose track of time watching it. For me, it was love at first sight.

In modern times, this crushing process is more frequently, and less romantically, accomplished by an automated roller mill. Roller mills are much more popular, and not just because they require less human—or beast—power to run; they're also much more efficient at extracting usable juice from the agave. (To produce one liter of tequila, for example, only five kilograms of roller-milled agave are needed, versus nearly ten kilograms of tahona-milled agave!)

Once the agave fibers are thoroughly shredded and crushed, water is added to the *mosto* to bring its sugars down to the right level, the *bagasso* is either separated out or mixed in, and we're ready for fermentation.

In huge vats known as *tinas*, which can be made out of quite literally anything, fermentation occurs. These days, stainless-steel tanks are most frequently used, but wood tanks, hollow tree trunks, clay pots, holes in the ground, and even animal-hide bags have been (and are) used to great effect. (There's an idiom in Mexico that I was told while sipping some particularly funky, sweet, leather-fermented mezcal in a Jaliscan *fabrica*: *Hasta las mañitas*— literally, "Up to the little hands"—which refers to someone who's very drunk. The phrase apparently comes from the days when agave spirits were often fermented in pigskin bags: a person who had imbibed a whole lot of hooch was said to have drunk everything *right up to the little hands*—that is, up to the pig's hooves, at the edges of the skin bag.)

Some producers add water to the fermentation vats immediately, while others wait for fermentation to get going strong first. The traditional way to make that happen is to allow the natural airborne yeasts unique to the area to start the fermentation, though some producers prefer to add their own yeast (natural or synthetic) in order to control the process more closely. Fermentation can last anywhere from a few days to a few weeks, depending on climate and ambient conditions, and what results is a low-proof beer of sorts.

If you stopped there, you'd have to drink a fair amount of the stuff to start feeling as if you could talk to the gods—and for some, the beverage itself might prevent you ever doing that. Pulque, a fermented agave beer, is an acquired taste. The drink can have mucus-y texture, akin to aloe juice, but it is wildly popular and people love the stuff. My favorite part of driving the Jaliscan roads to the Tequila valley are the little stands selling plastic jugs of it.

Because making agave spirits is such an old practice, the spirits are distilled using many different methods and types of still, including, copper alembic stills, wooden and clay stills, and, sometimes, unconventional column stills. Sometimes the *bagasso* is retained through the distillation process for additional flavor, but frequently it isn't, as it makes cleaning the still really annoying. Agave spirits are most often distilled twice—both mezcal and tequila must be, by law—but some producers stop after the first distillation. This first distillate, referred to as the *ordinario*, can come out to around 37 percent ABV. (And sometimes higher: there are some single-distillation *mezcales* from the region between Jalisco and Michoacan that come out to an impressive 46 percent!) Distilling it for a second time will bring it up as high as 55 percent ABV. Then, it can go to a bottle or to a barrel.

AGE STATEMENTS IN AGAVE SPIRITS

BLANCO or **PLATA**—meaning "white" or "silver"—is essentially unaged. These spirits must be bottled within sixty days of distillation.

REPOSADO—"rested"—is aged at least two months in oak.

AÑEJO—"aged"—spends at least one year in oak.

EXTRA AÑEJO is "extra aged" for at least three years, in barrels no larger than six hundred liters.

ORO—meaning "gold"—is not usually aged (contrary to what its appearance would suggest), but gets its coloration from additives and it's probably a mixto. The term **JOVEN**—or "young"—is used to mean this in tequila as well. (Confusingly, it is also used in mezcal to designate an unaged spirit—which is what most good mezcal is.)

With agave spirits, these rules only go one way. In other words, I can't call a tequila Añejo if it's only nine months old, but I can call my two-year-old spirit Reposado, if I want to. It's something that's rare in the spirits world, but fun—and provides some of the cheekier producers the opportunity to give a little "F-you" to an overbearing system. The Siembra Azul Suro Reposado, in which a number of Extra Añejos are blended and simply called "rested," is the best example of this.

One last, particularly ridiculous new category of tequila is worth mentioning here, if only to dismiss it: the so-called cristalino tequila that's been popping up in stores lately. **CRISTALINO** tequila is made by aging a tequila and then charcoal-filtering out the color and flavor that the aging process imparted to it, to make it clear again! Huh? Why go to all the trouble to make an Añejo and then waste time and money turning it back into a (less-flavorful) Blanco?

Agave fields at sunset. Santo Domingo de Albarradas, Oaxaca, Mexico.

LEGAL ISSUES

"The shameful thing is that a DO is supposed to protect the quality, the tradition, and the people who make it. But that's not happening."

—MISTY KALKOFEN, DEL MAGUEY

As I mentioned earlier, many Latin American spirits are just beginning to be recognized around the world, and as that recognition grows and the demand for these spirits in the global market grows with it, new laws often arise within these spirit-producing countries to regulate their production and consumption. Inevitably these laws create problems, particularly when they are used to regulate traditions (like those of agave spirits) that go back hundreds of years or more.

As was reinforced for me many times on my travels, it is impossible to talk about agave spirits today without talking about their laws and regulations, and the complex relationship that producers have to them. When I traveled in Mexico, I ended up discussing these topics everywhere I went—from a lunch at Cascahuin Tequila with agave activists and cultural anthropologists to mezcal-drunk nights in dusty *palenques* with families of *mezcaleros*. In Mexico, the laws of agave spirits, though relatively new, are on everyone's lips.

Tequila was *the* pioneering Latin spirit in terms of industrialization. As such, for better and worse, its regulatory laws have established the model for all other agave spirits that have followed, including mezcal; so it makes sense to talk about these laws first.

Tequila's rise in quality, and concurrent rise in popularity, came about thanks in large part to its strict regulatory standards. Tequila's DO, established in 1974, is today overseen by the Consejo Regulador del Tequila (CRT). Tasked with upholding the standards, image, and (perhaps most important) sales of tequila, the CRT works hard to keep everything in check—and they do it *every day*. That's right: *every single day* a member of the CRT checks in on *every single stage* of tequila production, *every single place* where it is officially undertaken. Because of this, tequila is one the most highly regulated spirits in the world today.

ENSAMBLES: THE RETURN OF THE ORIGINAL MEZCAL

Different agaves are used for spirits in different areas of Mexico (and beyond, too!), and nowadays a lot of mezcal producers even let you know right on the label which particular type of agave their mezcal is made from. But this single-agave type of mezcal is a relatively recent development in the spirit's history, likely begun in emulation of "single-source" spirits elsewhere. The original mezcal, so to speak, was something else.

Originally, back when all agaves were wild and production scales were much smaller, mezcal (and even tequila) was produced from a mix of whatever agaves in the area happened to be ripe when the local *mezcalero* needed them. These *ensamble* mezcales, as they're now called, made for interesting, ever-changing flavor profiles.

Today, *ensambles* are still made, though not as often as single-agave mezcales. *Mezcaleros* often use them as opportunities to create more complex spirits, showcasing different agaves' complementary qualities. Usually the *piñas* of different agaves are roasted and fermented together before being made into an *ensamble*, but in some cases, different single-agave spirits are separately distilled and then blended. As with the creation of an acholado-style Peruvian pisco, or any number of blended rums, there is a real art to this blending process in any case, and some of the finest mezcales out there are *ensambles*. Another reason to let go of our expectations of sameness and simplicity with these spirits!

The main purpose of all this oversight is to ensure that producers and bottlers adhere to the rules contained in the Norma Oficial Mexicana (NOM). These rules are many, but one of their outcomes—which guides consumers through at least one step in selecting a good tequila—is that legally, every bottle of tequila must be branded with a CRT logo and a four-digit NOM number. This NOM designation can tell you in what distillery a given spirit is produced and also helps you figure out what other spirits are also produced in that distillery. And be aware: if a shady, no-good, bad-tasting tequila is made at a distillery where other brands are also made, the same shade may well be thrown on those other tequilas, however pricey or in-demand they may be.

Legal regulation, though it has been part of tequila's heritage for a while now, has not by any means been seen as uniformly beneficial. Yes, it has made it possible for tequila to be protected as a product and to assume a place of great cultural importance for Mexico. But it has also led to the category becoming too narrow in some areas and too broad in others. Tequila's DO laws have often come about at the request, and to the benefit, of individual well-connected producers; and certain laws—the decision to allow diffusers in tequila production, for example—have been widely criticized as sacrificing the traditional integrity of the spirit in an effort to line the pockets of a select few.

"The changes that we have had to make to our mezcales, which break our traditions, are due to the laws of the CRM—if we don't make those changes, we can't bottle and sell. What the laws give us is a label that we can show to people who don't know us, to prove we're authentic. But what they're taking away, a lot of the time, is our authenticity. If there's no tradition, there's no mezcal."

—VICENTE SANCHEZ PARADA, REY CAMPERO

When mezcal was granted its own DO in 1994, the regions of production, methods of making, and types of agave legally associated with mezcal were narrowed down drastically, with both positive and negative results. On the positive side, it was no longer so easy for shady producers to pass off any old distillate as mezcal, and some of the lesser-known places where it was traditionally produced finally got some of the attention they deserved.

But for its benefits, mezcal's DO also cut out a *lot* of people. Many states that had been producing mezcal for centuries were now legally excluded from calling their product by that name and thus robbed of a major part of their cultural heritage—and mezcal, that vast and various family of agave spirits, was confined within a set of parameters that would prove increasingly troublesome to producers as the years went on. Today, the legal debate over mezcal's definition is a heated one, involving issues ranging from where mezcal can technically be *from* to what mezcal actually *is*. All of these arguments are overseen by the Consejo Regulador de Mezcal (CRM), a council founded in 1997 that deals exclusively with agave distillates produced by DO-regulated states as "mezcal." If this sounds familiar, that's because it is. In aim and methodology, the CRM is essentially a carbon copy of tequila's regulatory body, the CRT. Mezcal, however, is in many ways a *much* more difficult-to-define spirit than tequila, and the controversy surrounding its legal regulation has been dramatic since the beginning.

Nowadays, most spirits-people think of mezcal as a smoky spirit, likely made from Espadin agaves somewhere in Oaxaca, Mexico. This description accurately sums up the majority of the mezcal market, despite the fact that mezcal can currently come from many other states, and be made out of dozens of other types of agave. Oaxaca boasts Mexico's most diverse, rich terrain, with more agaves native to its soil than to all of the rest of the country: 95 percent of all *mezcales* do indeed come from Oaxaca, and the highest concentration of registered mezcal distilleries are found there. If you go there to visit some of these distilleries, you'll find the type of scene you'd expect to see anywhere that agriculture drives the economy: rows and rows of cultivated agaves, most of them Espadin, stretching out over hills in every direction as far as you can see. It looks, in short, quite a bit like the Tequila Valley—which makes sense, given mezcal's tequila-like rise in popularity.

Pot stills on the tropical grounds of Mezcal Tosba. Cajonos-Villa Alta, Oaxaca, Mexico.

CULTURAL HERITAGE IN AGAVE NAMES

It would seem that the most precise way to classify agaves would be the way a biologist would do it: by family, genus, and species. For broad purposes, this is true. But, even this supposedly objective system is not without its problems—especially when employed by a new industry like that of mezcal, in which attempts to simplify a product for legal regulation and global consumption can run counter to the preservation of its cultural heritage.

Trying to sum up that kind of cultural importance, even in terms of language, can be very difficult in Mexico. Consider this: in Oaxaca alone, sixteen languages are spoken, each with multiple dialects. When we visited Rey Campero, in Oaxaca's Candelaria Yegolé, everyone there was of Spanish mestizo descent and spoke Spanish. When we visited Santo Domingo de Albarradas, just a couple of hours away, everyone was of native descent and spoke Zapotec. Between these two *palenques*, different words were used for almost everything. And even within a number of different neighboring Zapotec communities, we found different phrases used for very common sayings. For example, the traditional Zapotec toast—more an expression of existential gratitude than a simple "cheers"—ranged from the well-known dixeebe ("DEESH-bay") to stigibeu ("stee-gee-BAY-oo") and stigibua'alu ("stee-gee-BWA-a-loo").

Agave names are no less variable. Papalome agaves, as they're called in Puebla, become Tobala agaves in Oaxaca; and what they call Largo in Oaxaca's Santa Catarina Minas is called Tobasiche just a few towns over. Agaves are also often locally named simply by their color (as with the blue agave), and this tradition can add considerably to the confusion involved in determining which agave is which. Different towns will call different agaves *cenizo*—"ash"—or *amarillo*—"yellow"—and the only thing that will connect the plants is the fact that they are genetically agaves with a particular hue to their *pencas*.

In these terms, the nomenclature of the CRM, which by necessity tries to narrow these names down to a single terminology, can amount to cultural whitewashing for those who end up forced to choose between their language and their livelihood. Graciela Angeles of Mezcal Real Minero put it very succinctly when I spoke with her while touring her nursery in Santa Catarina Minas: "When a town loses its language, it loses its culture. That's what the CRM has done, in many cases; it's taken our words. A wealth of language is needed to speak of cultural diversity, but when we all speak the same words and wear the same clothes, what cultural significance does the world have anymore? If mezcal loses this kind of cultural essence, it will cease to exist."

We are now seeing more and more mezcal coming from the other DO-recognized states; and with the increasing popularity of mezcal worldwide, the list itself seems likely to continue to grow. This expansion of recognized mezcal-producing regions, like other aspects of mezcal's DO, invites all sorts of complications—not least among them the fact that as mezcal becomes more profitable, more and more people who are getting into the game have little or no expertise with traditional mezcal-making practices. Even within some of the states recognized by mezcal's DO, only certain *towns* have historically made mezcal; but others, lured by the promise of quick profits, are quickly jumping on board.

This is not to say that there aren't new producers who are doing things very well. Working on sheer passion, cousins Elisandro Gonzalez-Molina and Edgar Gonzalez-Ramirez of Tosba Mezcal painstakingly learned the traditions of Oaxacan mezcal making, started their own *palenque* in the hills of the Sierra Norte, and are trying to incorporate ancient techniques from other areas into their production, using materials they grow and/or locally source. When I visited, we ate food hunted and grown on their land; even their distillery and farmhouse were beautifully hand built. Rather than being limited to their own personal history, they have been inspired by the traditions of others—and they approach these traditions with great respect, so they're able to do it right.

THE OTHERS: SOTOL, COMITECO, BACANORA, AND RAICILLA

Sure, we know about tequila and mezcal. But there's a whole other world of Mexican spirits out there, both agave-based and not, with and without legal recognition, to which a whole other book should be written. Among the non-agave-based spirits produced in Mexico are sugarcane aguardientes and some interesting eaux de vie made from tropical fruits, like mangos. Of agave distillates, it sometimes seems as if every region in Mexico has a different one, each with its own history and name: *barranca, tuxca, quitúpan, sikua* . . . the list goes on and on. (And that's just within Mexico; Venezuelans, for example, have their own agave spirit, *cocuy*!)

One Mexican spirit that's been commanding more attention lately is made from a plant not actually in the agave family at all, though the spirit is nevertheless frequently lumped in under the blanket term of mezcal. This delicious juice is called sotol. The spirit takes its name from its source plant, also called the desert spoon or Dasylirion, which is actually more closely related to an evergreen shrub than to agave. Visually, however, the two plants are very similar, and sotol was even miscategorized as an agave until DNA testing came along to tell us that in fact, they're just very similar-looking. Archeological remains of sotol ovens are said to have been found in the area of Paquíme in Casa Grandes, possibly dating back to the first century AD—providing a major source of support for pre-Hispanic distillation. Whether or not this is true, sotol distillation was widespread among the Spanish colonists in the mid-sixteenth century, and the spirit has been used by indigenous peoples in religious ceremonies and as a medicinal remedy for centuries.

Another interesting Mexican spirit is *comiteco*: a largely unknown agave spirit made in the southern state of Chiapas, from a maguey of the same name. The indigenous population of this area, the Tojolabal people, first drank the fermented agave juice from which they then distilled the spirit, and the fun fact about comiteco lies in the way that juice is gathered. Unlike the other agave distillates we've discussed here, with comiteco the agave is not roasted before fermentation, but instead the *aguamiel* of the agave is gathered separately by deeply slicing the *pencas* and *piña*, agitating the incisions each day, to produce sweet juice until the agave is effectively bled dry.

Bacanora is also a lesser-known agave Angustifolia distillate, hailing from the northern Mexican state of Sonora. Bacanora began as a *pulque* made by the indigenous Opata people in the Sonoran Desert and, like all the other Mexican distillates, has risen and fallen in popularity and clout within Mexico. Currently, it is hard to get outside of Mexico, even though it has its own DO, but it makes for fantastic cocktails, if you can get yourself a bottle.

Raicilla, an agave distillate produced in the state of Jalisco, has long been eclipsed by the tremendous success of the region's more famous spirit, tequila. Beyond the blue agave, Jalisco is actually home to a huge abundance of agave species—in fact, it's second only to Oaxaca in this respect—and because of this, as well as a lack of restrictions on how raicilla can be made and the great diversity of terroir to be found in the places it can be made in, raicilla has great variety in flavor. Raicilla producers are currently fighting for their own DO, and as always, there are arguments for and against it. One of the most compelling arguments against granting the DO is that it will bastardize the spirit by overgeneralizing what it is: to grant the name "raicilla" to any spirit from the state of Jalisco, for example, stretches the raicilla-making region far beyond the small coastal part of the state from which it traditionally comes. This has certainly been one of the outcomes of mezcal's controversial DO, and many people see raicilla's proposed DO as the sign of a troubling trend of cultural watering down.

Zulema Arias and Pedro Jiménez Guirría inside the agave-distillate mecca that is Mezonte Mezcalería. Guadalajara, Jalisco, Mexico.

The opposite side of this coin, of course, is that many people *do* have mezcal making in their history, and they want that history to be protected. "The DO is one of the most important things mezcal has right now," says Rómulo Sanchez Parada of mezcal producer Rey Campero. "But all the adding of new states that's going on right now—that has to do more with political and economic interests than with history and cultural importance. Yes, some areas of these states have a history of mezcal making, but rarely the entire state."

Narrowing down many production methods and materials to a single legal definition is no less problematic. Even the terminology used for the agaves can vary widely from one town, *palenque*, or *fabrica* to another. Variety is traditional to the practice of making mezcal—and attempts by the CRM to limit and regulate it strike many as countercultural. "The only advantage the DO grants *mezcaleros* is the right to put the word *mezcal* on their labels," says Mezonte's Pedro Jimenez Guirria. "But that's a right they should have earned simply by being mezcal producers, long before the creation of the DO. They shouldn't be fighting for that cultural element or having to pay a subscription to the CRM for it. It was already theirs."

A particularly nasty mezcal debate raged recently over proposition NOM 199, a widely reviled law under which any agave distillates not falling under DO definitions would have to be called *komil*—a word allegedly from the Nahuatl language (but whose authenticity is questioned by many scholars) referring simply to any intoxicating drink lacking distinction, like our word *booze*. Essentially, under this law, if you were a distiller who didn't live in the right place or have enough money, you wouldn't be legally allowed to call your spirit "mezcal"—or even put the words *agave* or *maguey* on your bottle. This obviously was met with resistance (and accusations of corruption), and in 2016 the proposition replaced the word *komil* with the phrase *Aguardiente de Agave*—which at least incorporated the word *agave*, but still was damaging to anyone who couldn't register their product as a mezcal due to geographic restrictions or lack of funds. Until recently, that is, where the term has been anarchically embraced.

Now, more producers are starting to bypass the legal regulations and opting to just have their spirits be called *Destilados de Agave*. This relatively new legislative term is allowing spirits previously unknown outside the villages in which they're made to be sold legally elsewhere within Mexico and abroad.

Some producers advocate for this to become the only legal designation within this family of spirits, which would mean saying good-bye to tequila and mezcal and their over-regulations, and hello to—well—anything you want. There's a valid argument here, I think; the term *Destilados de Agave* seems neutral enough to cover every agave spirit we need and limits fighting over nomenclature while allowing a wider diversity of Mexican producers to market their products and save legal fees. And it protects against the cultural watering down that tequila and mezcal have suffered from. As David Suro told me, "We've been doing such a good job hurting the categories of tequila and mezcal, there's now more respectability to be found in *Destilados de Agave*."

But there's a downside to the term, too: it potentially opens up the market to knockoffs. Since the phrase *Destilados de Agave* is not protected, anyone could distill agaves in any way they wanted, and sell their product as that—as originally happened with mezcal, before the term was legally regulated.

During this *Destilado de Agave* and *komil* debate, in early 2017, another big fight arose. This time it was in regard to the quietly passed NOM 70, which remains in effect as of this writing. This law defines the methods in which mezcal can be made, using a new set of categorizations that producers must print on their labels. That may not sound so bad in itself, but the law already has had some very serious ramifications. (One of its more unfortunate effects on the industry has been that, in classifying the diffuser as one of the legitimate methods of mezcal production, it gave big producers the go-ahead to pump out soulless, relatively tasteless juice and sell it under the same name as the robust, delicious drink that people have been making for centuries.)

So in the end, with legal loopholes such as these being created and abused under our noses, how can mezcal consumers ensure they are getting a good product? The key lies in better educating ourselves about what means what on a label. Under the current DO restrictions, mezcal must now be labeled according to three categories, which, as a basic rule, we can list from richest to poorest in cultural and agricultural terroir: *Mezcal Ancestral, Mezcal Artesanal,* and simply *Mezcal*.

Many mezcal geeks out there would likely define *Mezcal Ancestral* as the best stuff. However, there are real exceptions: I know of some *Mezcal Ancestral* producers who are working in an industrial fashion with dozens of clay Filipino stills at once, pumping out many thousands of liters every year. Is this consistent with the legal requirement of a "clay-pot still"? Sure. Is it consistent with the romantic vision most of us are paying for when we buy *Mezcal Ancestral*? Not at all—and it infuriates the purists that the two are confused. (I can certainly understand that; the traditional pot stills I've seen, prided by the people of towns such as Santa Catarina Minas, are sculptures to behold.)

THE WORM MYTH

Back in the day, the sentiment echoed by gringos everywhere was, "Oh, mezcal! The stuff with the worm in it!" Luckily, in the later part of the twenty-first century, common knowledge has broadened, and we're aware of the spirit as being much more than that. But . . . what's up with the worm?

That worm, called a *gusano*, is actually the larva of a moth species (and sometimes of a butterfly or weevil species) that preys on agaves. No one really knows where the weird tradition of adding the critters to bottles of mezcal began, but competing stories range from some kind of sick marketing ploy to the worm being pitched as an aphrodisiac to it simply being a mistake that had to be embraced in order to sell the product.

In any case, it's safe to say that if you want the good stuff, you shouldn't be drinking mezcal with any sort of bugs in it. (And while we're at it, it doesn't make you hallucinate to drink mezcal, with or without the worm. *Mescaline*, which definitely will make you hallucinate, is a totally different thing.)

Additionally, the term *Ancestral* really only applies to the ancestral traditions of some mezcal-producing states; in fact, if we're being honest, it more or less only applies to Oaxaca's. And again, on the flipside, since the category was created, a lot of people who never used clay-pot stills before, or never learned how to use them properly, have been picking them up, leading to the inevitable dilution of the category.

With its vastly inclusive definition, *Mezcal Artesanal* is the category that applies to most of the mezcal you've (hopefully) seen or tasted. And sure, it's nice for producers that it's not too difficult to obtain this status. But the definition of *Mezcal Artesanal* is *so* broad that many people (including me) think that there should be another category between it and Ancestral, to distinguish, say, the truly "artisanal" methods from others that weren't around before the twentieth century. (Mechanical shredder, anyone?)

The biggest downer comes with the last and least meaningful of these categories: the one, ironically, that ended up with the name *Mezcal*. Uneducated consumers who hear about mezcal and want to try it will probably buy the first (and probably cheapest) thing they find with "Mezcal" on the label. Unfortunately, now that diffuser-made spirits can be labeled this way, and Mezcal producers can cut corners by cooking agave *juices* rather than the agaves themselves, what you're likely to get when you buy this type of product is (to put it as kindly as possible) *not* the real deal. This "efficient" method of spirit making has taken its toll on tequila's heritage already; it would be a sad outcome if it ended up doing the same to mezcal.

CURRENT MEZCAL LABEL CATEGORIES AND THEIR MEANINGS

MEZCAL ANCESTRAL Agave hearts must be roasted in an underground stone oven; crushed by hand, with a stone molino, or with a Chilean or Egyptian mill; fermented in stone, earth, wood, or clay containers, or in animal skins, with agave fibers included; and distilled (again with fibers included) over direct fire, in a clay-pot still.

MEZCAL ARTESANAL Agave hearts must be roasted in an underground stone oven or aboveground masonry oven; crushed by hand, with a stone molino, with a Chilean or Egyptian mill, or with a crusher or shredder; fermented in stone, earth, wood, or clay containers, or in animal skins, with agave fibers included; and distilled (again with fibers included) over direct fire, in a copper alembic or clay-pot still.

MEZCAL Agave hearts or juice must be cooked in underground stone ovens, aboveground masonry ovens, or autoclaves; hearts must be crushed by hand, with a stone molino, with a Chilean or Egyptian mill, with an industrial crusher or shredder, or in a continuous mill, or processed with a diffuser; mosto must be fermented in wood, concrete, or stainless-steel tanks, and distilled in a pot or column still.

MARGARITA

1½ oz tequila of
your choice

¾ oz Cointreau

¾ oz lime juice

¼ oz Simple Syrup
(see page 243)

Lime wheel for garnish

Salt for garnish

While many, many tequila cocktails are worthy of the same kind of reverence as the margarita, we can thank this Latin American classic for putting agave on the classic-cocktail map. And that it certainly has done: the margarita is arguably one of the most popular drinks of all time, poured the world over.

Unfortunately, like everything popular, it's easily butchered. (I'm looking at you, sour mix and cheap tequila!) Some bartenders also like to put an insane amount of booze in their margaritas—as in three full ounces of 40 percent ABV spirit. I make mine less powerful and more balanced because I personally like to have a few of them at one sitting, because . . . they're delicious! Made right, the margarita is the perfect harmony of agave, lime, and triple sec (and when it comes to the latter, I find there is absolutely no substitute for Cointreau).

Add the tequila, Cointreau, lime juice, and simple syrup to a cocktail shaker with ice. Wet the outside of a rocks glass with the lime wheel and roll half the glass in salt for a half-salted rim. Shake and strain over fresh ice into the glass. Garnish with the lime wheel in the glass.

HAIL MARY

1 oz Siete Leguas
Tequila Blanco

¾ oz Salers Aperitif

½ oz lemon juice

½ oz Raspberry Syrup
(recipe follows)

¼ oz Giffard Creme
de Peche

1 dash Regan's
Orange Bitters

2 oz Raventós i Blanc
de Nit Rosado Cava

Grapefruit twist
for garnish

If you get the chance, you must go to the churchlike shrine of Siete Leguas's new distillery in Jalisco. Stained-glass windows bathe the entire space with a warm glow, while horses circle languidly around *tahonas*, and gorgeous copper stills reflect the light. It's like a cathedral, an art museum, and a traditional distillery all in one, and it's absolutely breathtaking.

This drink, for me, is the one to drink in such a place. I love bubbles, and I love riffing on sparkling-wine drinks. There are a lot of them out there; probably the best known is the French 75, to which I pay homage here. This drink takes its lead from the blanco tequila of Siete Leguas, with its rich fruit; I decided to add a touch of bittersweet Salers Aperitif to combat the sweeter fruit flavors and tie into the sparkling wine for a little more dryness.

Add all the ingredients, except the cava and grapefruit twist, to a cocktail shaker with ice. Shake and fine-strain into a coupe glass. Top with the cava. Express the grapefruit twist over the drink and then rest the twist on the rim.

RASPBERRY SYRUP

1 cup raspberries

2 cups granulated sugar

1 cup water

MAKES 1 QT • Place the ingredients in a blender and blend on high speed until the contents are well integrated. Pour through a chinois strainer to remove solids and transfer to an airtight container. Store in the refrigerator for up to 2 weeks.

PALOMA

2 oz tequila of
your choice

¾ oz lime juice

¾ oz grapefruit juice

¾ oz Simple Syrup
(see page 243)

Lime wheel for garnish

Salt for garnish

1 oz club soda

Grapefruit wheel, halved,
for garnish

Traditionally, this classic Mexican cocktail is made with grapefruit soda—generally Squirt. (I also like mine made with the zesty Jamaican Ting.) But freshness is key at Leyenda, so we like to do ours the natural way, with fresh juices. It's a drink that really comes alive. Try it with mezcal, try it with jalapeño-infused tequila—it's good with just about anything!

Add the tequila, both juices, and simple syrup to a cocktail shaker with ice. Wet the rim of a Collins glass with the lime wheel and roll in salt for a salt rim. Shake and strain over fresh ice into the glass. Top with the club soda. Garnish with the lime and grapefruit wheels.

CABEZAZO

1 oz Jameson Black Barrel
Irish Whiskey

¾ oz Del Maguey
Vida Mezcal

¾ oz Lillet Rose Aperitif

¾ oz Martini & Rossi
Bianco Vermouth

1 tsp St. Germain
Elderflower Liqueur

3 dashes Bittermans
Hellfire Habanero Shrub

3 dashes Bittermans
Mole Bitters

Lemon twist for garnish

On one infamous trip to Oaxaca, at one particular cantina, a group of us were playing dice in a corner when a man walked up to the bar, ordered a drink, and, when it came, suddenly headbutted the young bartender. He then left his drink on the bar and walked right out. The music didn't even stop, and no one seemed to care or notice—except the bartender with his bloody nose. This drink, whose name means "headbutt," is a tribute to that bizarre night.

Add all the ingredients, except the lemon twist, to a mixing glass with ice. Stir and strain into a Nick and Nora glass. Express the oils of the lemon twist over the glass and then float the twist in the drink.

TIA MIA

1 oz Del Maguey Chichicapa Mezcal

1 oz Appleton Reserve Rum

½ oz Pierre Ferrand Orange Curaçao

¾ oz lime juice

½ oz Orgeat Works T'Orgeat Toasted Almond Syrup

Mint sprig for garnish

Lime wheel for garnish

Edible orchid for garnish (optional)

Being a mezcal lover, I went through a phase where I tried floating mezcal on top of all sorts of different drinks. This drink is the first cocktail I ever put on one of Julie Reiner's menus when I worked at Lani Kai in 2010. It continues to remain a staple on the menu at Leyenda.

I started by floating an ounce of mezcal on top of my Mai Tai (see page 145) and then swapped out the funky rhum agricole we used in our recipe there altogether by replacing it with the smoky and equally funky mezcal. The result was the Tia Mia, whose name is an anagram of its namesake (the mai tai) and an homage to my friend Catherine, my *Tia de Alma* ("spiritual aunt," i.e., close, but not related by blood), who was my bar regular when I bartended in Guatemala.

Add the mezcal, rum, curaçao, lime juice, and orgeat to a cocktail shaker with ice. Shake briefly and strain over crushed or pebbled ice in a large rocks glass. Traditionally, we garnish this drink at Leyenda with a mint sprig, a lime wheel, and an edible orchid for fun flair, but if you can't get your hands on an orchid, don't worry! It's only there to add a beautiful touch to the cocktail.

GHOST COAST

1 oz Tromba
Reposado Tequila

½ oz Tapatio 110
Tequila Blanco

½ oz Giffard Crème
de Banane

¼ oz Eucalyptus Tincture
(recipe follows)

¾ oz lemon juice

½ oz Honey Syrup
(see page 241)

¼ oz maple syrup

2 dashes Angostura
Aromatic Bitters

Eucalyptus leaf for garnish

Banana chip for garnish

Jesse Harris created this Leyenda classic as an homage to his home on the California coast, where eucalyptus trees line the beaches. The reposado tequila is given a punch-up with the higher-proof blanco tequila, providing the drink with a backbone to hold up the strong flavors within it. This one's truly one of my all-time favorites.

Add all the ingredients, except the eucalyptus leaf and the banana chip, to a cocktail shaker with ice. Shake and strain into a rocks glass over fresh ice. Garnish with the eucalyptus leaf and the banana chip on a pick.

EUCALYPTUS TINCTURE

2 oz (by weight) eucalyptus
leaves, washed

9 oz water

9 oz Polmos Spirytus
Rektyfikowany or other
everclear alcohol

MAKES 20 OZ • Combine the eucalyptus and alcohol in a quart-size container. Let sit covered in open air for 36 hours. Strain, add the water, and bottle. Store in the refrigerator indefinitely.

CAPATÁZ

1¼ oz Del Maguey
Vida Mezcal

1¼ oz Cesar Florido
Fino Sherry

¾ oz Cesar Florido
Moscatel Sherry

¼ oz Suze

1 tsp Giffard Crème
de Banane

Lime twist for garnish

5 to 6 spritzes Del Maguey
Santo Domingo de
Albarradas Mezcal

Tom Macy, one of my business partners at Leyenda, created this drink. He was inspired by Del Maguey's Santo Domingo de Albarradas mezcal, a rich and slightly bitter spirit with notes of super fruit and funk. Tom's cocktail is structured almost like a Manhattan, with a blend of sherries in lieu of vermouth, Vida mezcal for backbone, a touch of Suze for bitterness, and banana liqueur for the fruit.

Add all the ingredients, except the lime twist and Santo Domingo de Albarradas mezcal, to a mixing glass with ice. Stir and strain into a rocks glass over a big ice cube. Express the oils of the lime twist over the glass and then place the twist between the cube and glass. Using an atomizer, spritz the Del Maguey Santo Domingo de Albarradas mezcal on top for aromatics.

¡BOLA BOLA!

¾ oz Mezonte Raicilla Tepe

¾ oz Plantation Barbados 5-Year Rum

½ oz Lustau Amontillado Sherry

¼ oz Ancho Reyes Liqueur

¾ oz lemon juice

½ oz Orgeat Works T'Orgeat Toasted Almond Syrup

½ tsp Tajín Classic Seasoning

Lemon wheel for garnish

Of all my favorite bars in the world, few compare to Pare de Sufrir (literally meaning, "Stop Suffering") in Guadalaja, Mexico, owned by agave specialist Pedro Jimenez Guirria. When you walk into this space, you're immediately greeted by the sight of hipster Mexican youth dancing and drinking beers and an array of awesome Mexican distillates, particularly from their own state of Jalisco. Apart from the choice spirits, the best part of this bar is the disco ball in the middle of the room, which, rather than being motor-operated, has to be spun with a broom handle by the busy bartenders to get it going. Whenever it stops spinning—which it does many times a night—chants rise up of "Bola! Bola!" (literally meaning, "[disco] ball, [disco] ball!").

This drink features a particularly excellent agave spirit made by a secretive indigenous population in the hills between Jalisco and Durango. It's a rare treat, really to be consumed neat and alone, with unique notes of apples, nuts, and bright vinegar. In honor of Pare de Sufrir, I decided to mix it up, just this once.

Add all the ingredients, except the Tajín Classic Seasoning and lemon wheel, to a cocktail shaker with ice. Shake and strain over fresh ice in a highball glass. Dust half the lemon wheel with the Tajín Classic Seasoning and rest on top of the ice.

WITCHING HOUR

1½ oz Sotol Por Siempre

¾ oz Von Humboldt's
Tamarind Cordial

¼ oz Dolin Blanc
Vermouth de Chambery

¼ oz Orgeat Works
T'Orgeat Toasted
Almond Syrup

¼ oz lemon juice

3 drops Bittermans
Orchard Street
Celery Shrub

Celery leaf for garnish

Sotol's unusual, aggressive flavor profile can be even trickier to use than mezcal, and it usually requires a little hand-holding on the part of the bartender to introduce properly. Leyenda's head bartender, Shannon Ponche went out on a limb when she created this delicious cocktail (pictured opposite), combating the vegetal asparagus notes of the sotol with a bit of tamarind liqueur to make this savory treat.

Add all the ingredients, except the celery leaf, to a mixing glass with ice. Stir and strain into a rocks glass over a big ice cube. Garnish with the celery leaf floating on the big cube.

SINKING STONE

1¼ oz Koch
Espadin Mezcal

½ oz Plantation
Jamaican Rum

½ oz Atxa Vino
Vermouth Blanco

½ oz Cynar

¼ oz Plantation
Pineapple Rum

Orange twist
for garnish

Frequently in the cocktail world, drinks imitate drinks imitate drinks—and this one is an adaptation of an adaptation of the Negroni. I liked the higher-proof mesquite notes of this particular espadin mezcal, and I wanted to heighten its slight bitterness and fruit notes. I elected to use a blend of rums and Spanish vermouth to accomplish this. This funky, earthy, bitter sipper brings in different fruit notes and a sweetness out of this complex mezcal.

Add all the ingredients, except the orange twist, to a mixing glass with ice. Stir and strain into a rocks glass over a big ice cube. Express the oils of the orange twist over the glass and rest the twist in the glass.

PERENNIAL MILLENNIAL

1¼ oz El Tesoro
Tequila Blanco

¼ oz Deniset-Klainguer
Fraise des Bois

½ oz Yellow Chartreuse

¼ oz Vanilla Syrup
(see page 243)

¾ oz Rhubarb Syrup
(recipe follows)

¾ oz lemon juice

½ tsp Campari

2 drops Saline Tincture
(see page 243)

Cucumber ribbon
for garnish

1 dash Cardamom Tincture
(see page 240)

This beautiful drink was created by Jesse Harris at Leyenda. Siete Leguas tequila has sweet, earthy notes that play up the rhubarb and vanilla, and the Chartreuse mellows it while the cardamom brings the acid back up. There's quite a bit of prep for this drink with the rhubarb syrup, but the result is worth it!

Add all the ingredients, except the cucumber ribbon and cardamom tincture, to a cocktail shaker with ice. Spiral the cucumber ribbon inside a pilsner or large Collins glass and then add crushed or pebbled ice. Add the cardamom tincture on top for aromatics.

RHUBARB SYRUP

½ lb rhubarb cut into
1-inch cubes

½ lb cleaned and
hulled strawberries

Zest and juice of 1 small orange
(yields ½ cup orange juice)

Zest of 1 lemon

1 cup superfine sugar

1 Tbsp vanilla extract

MAKES I QT · Mix all the ingredients together in a saucepan and simmer over low heat for 20 minutes. Remove from the heat and allow to cool. Blend with an immersion blender and then transfer to an airtight container. Store in the refrigerator for up to 4 weeks.

PALO NEGRO

2 oz Partida
Reposado Tequila

1 oz Lustau Palo
Cortado Sherry

½ oz Cruzan
Blackstrap Rum

1 tsp Demerara Syrup
(see page 241)

1 tsp Grand Marnier

Orange twist for garnish

This is a great fall or winter slow-sipper that is rich and complex, celebrating the aged tequila and rich sherry. I created this drink to remember a particularly cool night I spent in the Tequila Valley, where we sipped reposado throughout "to keep warm." The black-pepper notes of Partida tequila cut nicely into the nutty sweetness of the sherry, and the blackstrap rum acts as a bridge between them. Who says tequila is just a summer drink?

Add all the ingredients, except the orange twist, to a mixing glass with ice. Stir and strain into a Nick and Nora glass. Express the oils of the orange twist over the glass and float the twist within.

SOUTH FENCE

4 slices cucumber

¾ oz El Jolgorio Espadin Mezcal

¾ oz jalapeño-infused Siembra Valles Blanco Tequila (see page 242)

¾ oz Lustau Amontillado Sherry

¾ oz lime juice

½ oz Agave Syrup (see page 240)

1 dash Bittermans Orchard Street Celery Shrub

1 oz soda water

Mint sprig for garnish

The drink's name refers to the infamous wall that the forty-fifth president of the United States was so keen on building. With it, I took the classic Southside cocktail (made with gin and muddled mint and cucumber) and put a spin on it, using a little sherry to give nuance to the drink and help link the mezcal to the cucumber and jalapeño.

Muddle 3 cucumber slices in a cocktail shaker. Add all the other ingredients, except the reserved cucumber slice, the soda water, and the mint, to a cocktail shaker with ice. Shake and fine-strain into a highball glass with fresh ice. Top with the soda water and garnish with the remaining cucumber slice with the mint sprig poked through the middle.

SAY ANYTHING

1 oz jalapeño-infused
Siembra Valles Blanco
Tequila (see page 242)

½ oz Novo Fogo
Silver Cachaça

½ oz Aperol

1 oz Watermelon Syrup
(recipe follows)

¾ oz lime juice

5 to 7 mint leaves

Lime wheel for garnish

Salt for garnish

I wanted to make the perfect romantic-comedy homage in a drink—a little sweet, a little bitter, and HOT. The inspiration for the Say Anything, a great little summer sipper, came about when I was doing a new menu tasting with the staff at Leyenda. As I was miming the classic moment in the movie of the same name, where John Cusack holds the boombox over his head, I suddenly realized that none of the young staff knew what I was talking about. Oh, youth!

Add all the ingredients, except for 1 mint leaf, the lime wheel, and salt, to a cocktail shaker with ice. Wet the outside of a coupe glass with the lime wheel and roll the glass in salt for a salted rim. Shake and fine-strain into the glass. Garnish with the mint leaf—first pressed lightly to express its oils— by floating it on top of the drink.

WATERMELON SYRUP

2 cups cubed seedless
watermelon

¾ cup superfine sugar

MAKES 2 CUPS · Blend the watermelon in a blender to yield about 12 ounces of juice. Add the sugar and blend again until fully dissolved. Transfer to an airtight container. Store in the refrigerator for up to 2 weeks.

CEREZA PICANTE

1 oz jalapeño-infused
Arette Blanco Tequila
(see page 242)

¾ oz Cherry
Heering Liqueur

½ oz Rey Campero
Espadin Mezcal

¾ oz lime juice

¼ oz Simple Syrup
(see page 243)

Lime wedge for garnish

Luxardo Maraschino
Cherry for garnish

When making the road trip from the Tequila Valley to the highlands, I like to stop and get sweets to pair with the occasional taco, *pulque*, or nip of tequila. My favorite kind of sweet, if I can find them, are these spicy cherry lollipops sold by kids on the road, right next to their *pulque*-selling parents. I made this drink to remind me of those funky sour sweets and bring me back when I'm too far away!

Add all the ingredients, except the lime wedge and cherry, to a cocktail shaker with ice. Shake and strain over fresh ice in a rocks glass. Garnish with the lime wedge and the cherry pierced on a cocktail pick.

FÍJATE

¾ oz Tosba
Pechuga Mezcal

¾ oz Neversink Spirits
Apple Aperitif

½ oz Fig-Infused Rancho
Tepua Bacanora Blanco
(recipe follows)

½ tsp Vicario Monk's
Secret Liqueur, plus
4 spritzes for garnish

2 dashes Saline Tincture
(see page 243)

1 dash Peychauds bitters

¼ fig for garnish

Pechuga mezcals are so full and vibrant that they practically beg to be made into drinks—though frequently their cost prohibits that. Here, I wanted to indulge and create a cocktail that played on their unique fruity and gamey flavors. Tosba Pechuga is made with a turkey breast hung above the distillation with lots of wild apples and pineapples—all of which are grown on the distillery's beautiful property in the misty mountains of northern Oaxaca. The apple aperitif acts like a fortified wine in the drink, and the Monk's liqueur, which has a fantastic churchlike incense taste to it, reinforces the mezcal's light smoke. Keep in mind: this recipe requires a longer infusion, so prep time is needed!

Add all the ingredients, except the fig, to a mixing glass with ice and then stir. Strain over a large ice cube in a rocks glass. Garnish with the fig and 4 spritzes of the Vicario Monk's Secret Liqueur on top.

FIG-INFUSED RANCHO TEPUA BACANORA BLANCO

5 medium figs

750 ml Rancho Tepua
Bacanora Blanco

MAKES 750 ML · Slice the figs and place in a small pan over medium heat until browned, 5 to 8 minutes, and let cool slightly. Muddle the figs in a food-safe container and add the Bacanora. Let sit for 8 hours, stirring occasionally. Pour through a chinois strainer to remove solids and bottle. Store in the refrigerator indefinitely.

ARINATO

1½ oz Ilegal Mezcal Joven

¾ oz Lillet Blanc

½ oz Dolin Dry Vermouth

¼ oz Yellow Chartreuse

½ tsp Luxardo
Maraschino Liqueur

2 dashes
Peychaud's Bitters

Grapefruit twist
for garnish

Mezcal can be a beast, and when it first came into popularity in the United States, that was a big part of its appeal. (So much smoke! So much flavor!) However, in drink making, sometimes too much is too much; and if you want to use mezcal as your base and not a modifier, it can easily drown out the rest of the drink. I created the Arinato to be a lighter stirred drink and to celebrate the more delicate sides of what many think of as a brutish spirit. The mezcal I use is the 80-proof Ilegal Joven; paired with floral fortified wines, it makes for an easy-sipper that proves how elegant mezcal can be.

Add all the ingredients, except the grapefruit twist, to a mixing glass with ice and stir. Strain over a large ice cube in a rocks glass. Express the grapefruit twist over the drink and then rest the twist on the cube in the glass.

POINT HIGHER

¾ oz El Tesoro Reposado

¼ oz Giffard
Caribbean Pineapple

½ oz Serrano Syrup
(recipe follows)

½ oz carrot juice

¾ oz lemon juice

Lemon wheel for garnish

On one trip to the La Alteña distillery years ago, we went to eat in my favorite carnitas spot, Carnitas Jaimes. (This is a MUST-stop if you ever make it up to the highlands of Jalisco! Not only is the food next level but mariachis serenade you while you eat and drink.) The drink of choice there is, obviously, tequila, which pairs awesomely with the pork and pickled carrots and serranos. This drink was conceptualized while we ate our weight in carnitas and drank tequila from the entire region. When I returned to Brooklyn, I created this drink, adding just a touch of crème de pineapple to the recipe to bring out some of the sweetness of the agave.

Add all the ingredients, except the lemon wheel, to a cocktail shaker with ice. Shake and fine-strain into a coupe glass. Garnish by floating the lemon wheel.

SERRANO SYRUP

4 serrano peppers
(preferably red or orange)

2 oz water

4 oz agave nectar

MAKES 8 OZ · Using a juicer, juice the serranos to yield approximately 2 oz. Be sure to wear gloves for cutting and wash knives and surfaces immediately. Add the water and nectar to the serrano juice. Stir to integrate, then fine-strain and bottle. Store in the refrigerator for up to 2 weeks.

AS SHE SO TOLD

¾ oz Clande Sotol Lot 2

¾ oz Fortaleza
Reposado Tequila

½ oz Wölffer Estate Verjus

½ oz Lo Fi Dry Vermouth

¼ oz Clear Creek
Douglas Fir Brandy

¼ oz chamomile syrup

1 dash Saline Tincture
(see page 243)

I have yet to visit Chihuahua's own sotol distilleries, only ever having skirted around the Mexican state while driving in the south of Texas (and peering thirstily over the border). Luckily, Clande's founder, Ricardo Pico, is a huge wealth of knowledge, and he is always happy to share random plastic bottles he's brought back, educating me and others on this unusual, mossy-yet-minty drink. Here, I wanted to highlight the rich fruits but oddly pinesap-like quality of this spirit, which reminds me of nights along the border, wanting to go out and explore.

Add all the ingredients to a mixing glass with ice and stir. Strain over a large ice cube in a rocks glass.

'LIL SMOKEY

2 lime wedges

5 sage leaves

¾ oz Pineapple Syrup
(see page 242)

1½ oz Ilegal Mezcal Joven

½ oz Novo Fogo
Silver Cachaça

½ oz lime juice

Seared pineapple wedge
for garnish

This is a drink created by the fantastically talented Shannon Ponche. She has mastered savory drinks better than anyone I know, and this refreshing, herbaceous cocktail is a great example. It's a play on the Caipirinha (see page 144) that incorporates some mezcal for added complexity but avoids drowning out the other flavors with smoke.

Add the lime wedges and 3 sage leaves to a cocktail shaker and muddle in the pineapple syrup. Add the spirits, lime juice, and ice. Shake hard and pour all the contents directly into a rocks glass. Garnish with the grilled pineapple wedge and remaining 2 sage leaves on a pick. (If you don't want to grill the pineapple, that's okay! But it makes for a nice look.)

BIG KARWINSKI

1 oz Siembra
Azul Reposado

½ oz Rey Campero
Madre Cuishe Mezcal

½ oz Mole Negro Kalvah
(recipe follows)

¼ oz oz J. Rieger & Co.
Caffè Amaro

Lightly whipped cream
for garnish

Cocoa powder for garnish

While visiting the fantastic people at Rey Campero in Candelaria Yegolé, Oaxaca, we found ourselves running through rows of Madrecuishe agave at sunset, screaming "Karwinski!" (This is a particularly Dr. Seuss–esque family of agaves, to which Madrecuixe belongs, that grow almost like a pineapple on a palm tree–like stalk; it's not hard to pick out their silhouettes against the sky.) I'd like to say that was before the drinking started, but really no time was before the drinking started on that trip to the arid Oaxacan South.

This drink is a riff on the White Russian—and its name, yes, is a *Big Lebowski* reference. Its flavors are meant to play up the fruit and light chocolate notes hiding behind the vegetal, split-wood greenness of the Madre Cuishe mezcal.

Add all the ingredients, except the whipped cream and cocoa powder, to a mixing glass with ice. Stir and strain into a rocks glass with fresh ice and add a float of whipped cream on top. Dust with cocoa powder.

MOLE NEGRO KALVAH

5 oz mole negro paste   750 ml Kahlua Coffee Liqueur

MAKES 1 QT · Combine the mole negro and Kahlua in a blender and blend until unified. Transfer to an airtight container. Store in the refrigerator indefinitely.

DOUBLE SALUTE

1¼ oz Michter's
Bourbon Whiskey

¾ oz Ilegal Mezcal Joven

¾ oz lemon juice

¾ oz Tumericane
(recipe follows)

½ oz Luxardo
Apricot Liqueur

½ oz red wine
(I suggest Grenache)

Freshly ground
black pepper for garnish

Alisha Neverson created this nice rich drink for Leyenda. The bourbon acts as a rich canvas to carry the slight smoke of the mezcal, which in turn gets a boost from the turmeric. The apricot liqueur used here is actually pretty bitter, pairing with the red-wine float and pepper to round everything out.

Add all the ingredients, except the wine and black pepper, to a cocktail shaker with ice. Shake and strain into a rocks glass over a big ice cube. Gently pour the red wine over the drink and finish with a light dusting of black pepper on top.

TUMERICANE

2 tsp powdered turmeric

1 cup water

2 cups cane sugar

MAKES 2 CUPS · Add the turmeric to the water and bring to a boil over high heat. Then add the sugar and turn the heat to medium, stirring until the sugar dissolves. Remove from the heat, allow to cool, and bottle. Store in the refrigerator for up 1 month.

ALTEÑA VIEJA

1 oz El Tesoro
Añejo Tequila

½ oz Knob Creek
Rye Whiskey

¼ oz Mace-Infused
Tapatio 110 Tequila Blanco
(recipe follows)

¼ oz Lustau
Moscatel Sherry

½ tsp Cinnamon Bark
Syrup (see page 241)

1 dash Regan's
Orange Bitters

Lemon twist for garnish

Orange twist for garnish

I have visited La Alteña distillery many times, starting with an epic trip for Tequila Ocho—which is made there—with co-founder Tomas Estes. Although Tomas is a foreigner, hailing from the United States and now living in London, he joined the multigenerational Camarena family at La Alteña to make his tequila; and on that first trip, I got to see the nuances of the distillery and, most important, their dedication to family and tradition. The family employs generations of different families at the distillery and in their agave fields; some stay their entire lives.

On my last visit there, nearly a decade later, this time with El Tesora, I saw a man I'd met on that first trip. Too old now to do much physical labor anymore, he's officially retired and comes into the distillery of his own accord to shine the stainless-steel holding tanks. This drink is for him.

Add all the ingredients, except the lemon and orange twists, to a mixing glass with ice. Stir and then strain into a rocks glass over a large ice cube. Express the oils of the lemon and orange twists over the glass and then add the twists to the glass.

MACE-INFUSED TAPATIO 110 TEQUILA BLANCO

10 oz Tapatio 110 Tequila Blanco   1 Tbsp dried and ground mace

MAKES 10 OZ · Combine the Tapatio and mace in a quart-size jar and let rest for 3 days unrefrigerated. Strain through a chinois and bottle. Store refrigerated indefinitely.

SUGAR-CANE

Above: Workers load hand-cut sugarcane into a truck. Appleton Estate, St. Elizabeth, Jamaica. **Page 102:** Valdemar Onisko and Emerson Santos harvesting sugarcane for Novo Fogo Cachaça. Morretes, Paraná, Brazil.

A bottle of rum, or a cocktail made from it, contains much more than a spirit made of sugarcane. Rum represents a truly complex blending of human histories—the result of colonization, yes, but also of the rise and fall of the slave trade, and the unique cultural melting pot that was produced in the Americas. The present-day outcome of this many-faceted history is that, unlike with many other spirits, rum really has no rules; it came about, and continues to exist, in its own ramshackle way. Everything about rum is both foreign and natural, exotic and familiar: the result of plants and people being moved from one place to another, and forced to coexist until that coexistence became the new normal.

In accounting for the cultural terroir of this chaotic spirit, in addition to the influences of Europe and of the indigenous peoples and climates of the Americas, we have a third crucial influence to factor in: the influence of Africa, first brought over in the form of enslaved human beings. This influence affected the back-and-forth of colonial Europe and indigenous America in complex, unpredictable ways—all of which have become an integral part of what we experience when we drink these spirits. In this sense, sugarcane distillates are the sweet taste of chaos, a celebration of variety and improvisation in the face of adversity.

The diverse cultural intermixtures that rum represents exist in the populations of the places best known for producing it. Just about all of the people in these areas—mainly the islands of the Caribbean and the mainland countries immediately surrounding them—are of some African descent, with quite a bit of European cultural influence present in the languages spoken, foods eaten, games played, and other traditions followed. Of course, the need for African slaves originated with the colonists, who virtually annihilated the indigenous populations they encountered—the Carib, Arawak, Taíno, and Warao peoples, among others—as they rushed to conquer new land. Even those natives who yielded to slavery were often quickly killed off by European-borne diseases, to which they had never developed an immunity. After this wipeout, the capture and export of African slaves came to be relied upon more heavily than ever among the European colonists, especially the sugarcane farmers; and as the West Indian sugar trade grew, the slave trade grew with it.

Around 70 percent of the estimated twelve million African people who were captured and brought over to the Americas were sent to sugarcane plantations across the Caribbean and the Americas. These people, stolen from all over Africa, represented vastly different racial, geographical, and cultural backgrounds. Motley new national identities were created among the slaves, their enslavers, and the remaining natives, mixing religions, dialects, and concepts from the various homelands of the islands' new inhabitants.

Rum, in its plural forms, is a chief example of the struggle its creators went through to adapt to their wildly different new surroundings. As the new identities of the islands and mainland were born, each according to its own norms and practices, each produced its own version of the sugarcane distillate to fit them, and an often self-contradictory family of spirits was created. Produced and enjoyed both as a proud embodiment of rural simplicity and as an ideal of high refinement, rum was embraced by rich, poor, and enslaved people alike, picking up different characteristics everywhere it took hold. It gained a foothold in Catholic communities, while becoming central to the rites of Voodoo and Santeria. It took on accents British and French, Spanish, Portuguese, and Dutch—always in its own creole—and these wildly different accents and usages persist in rum today.

So how exactly did these differences come to be? Why are some Jamaican rums so wonderfully funky, or Cuban rums so delicately light? What are rhum agricole and cachaça, and what gives them their unique flavors? To answer these questions, it will be necessary to delve first into the history of the sugarcane industry, that enormous global force that almost single-handedly brought rum, and the unique Latin cultures it represents, into being.

HISTORY

Sugarcane is not a native to the Americas, but it would find the ecosystem of its dreams when colonists brought it to the Caribbean. Unlike the agaves indigenous to Mexico, the sweet, bamboo-like grass originated in New Guinea, where the first sugarcane crops are thought to have been cultivated as early as 8000 BC. Its journey to this other hemisphere was long and arduous.

Once sugar's popularity had taken off in India, where the milling and refining process that made sugar transportable was first developed, the product spread west: first to Persia and then to Europe via Arab and Moorish traders and Crusaders returning from the Middle East. Of course, the cane itself didn't grow as readily in the brisker climates of Europe as it had in India or New Guinea, so sugar remained a luxury in Europe for quite a while. Until the early eleventh century, sugar was still thought of as an exotic spice, arriving occasionally with others from the Far East. And it was astronomically expensive; until around the seventeenth century, a single gram would have set you back the modern-day equivalent of $10. (Think about that the next time you're putting a lump or two in your coffee!)

The Portuguese were the first to migrate sugarcane west to the "new world" of the Americas, with the Spanish not far behind. Harvesting the tough canes and stripping off their fibrous outer parts to get at their sweet centers is hard manual labor; so as soon as European colonists began farming sugarcane on a large scale, they began to look around for people to do it for them as cheaply as possible. Their answer was African slaves. When the Portuguese landed in Madeira, off the coast of Morocco, and the Spanish found the Canary Islands, they both found great sugarcane-growing lands there, and they imported African slaves from the mainland to do the work. In 1444, the first slaves were shipped over to work the Madeiran sugar fields, and the international sugar trade found its longtime partner in African slavery.

It wasn't until the "discoverer" of the Americas, Christopher Columbus, took sail to try to break Spain into the spice-trade game in the East Indies, that this ugly new partnership made it to Latin America. What we now know is that Columbus's plan to head west on what he thought was a short-cut to Asia landed him smack in the West Indies (which he thought was India), where he first made landfall in the Bahamas and then went onward to Hispaniola (the island comprising modern-day Haiti and the Dominican Republic). Rightly believing Hispaniola to be agriculturally plentiful and capable of great abundance, Columbus established his first colony there. On his second journey in 1493, he brought back cane sprouts from his wife's Canary Island plantation, and the attempt to produce sugar in this new ecosystem began. Since then, an intensely active few hundred years have proven what those early West Indian sugar farmers suspected: sugarcane had finally found its ideal home in the gates of this so-called New World: the Caribbean.

Though Columbus was happy with how well sugarcane took to the islands, it was primarily precious metals he was really looking for, so he left the plush surrounds of the West Indies and sailed farther south and west, going on to "discover" Central and South America. Spain's general lack of interest in protecting its findings made it easy for other European colonial powers to follow in Columbus's wake, all of whom claimed other islands as their own and established farms, ports, and settlements there. Soon there were French, Portuguese, Dutch, and English colonies in the West Indies, too, all racing to profit from the unprecedented agricultural bounty of the tropics. Sugar, previously a luxury reserved for the very rich, quickly became a European commonplace as the West Indian sugar trade boomed, nurtured on stolen land with the blood and toil of stolen people. Caribbean settlers started to sell the sugar, and then the spirits made from it, back to their partners in Africa and Europe in exchange for more African slaves, who were then shipped back and forced to make more of the juice that had brought them there in the first place. The so-called Middle Passage—the marine pathway between the new lands—would be the route along which millions of displaced Africans would be shackled and shuttled over the next four hundred years.

With active trade routes, abundant fertile land, and what seemed to be an endless supply of slaves to farm it, the growing demand for the world's most exciting new sweetener was met vigorously. With so much sugarcane juice flowing—and quickly fermenting in the hot climate—it didn't take long for people, probably the Portuguese first, to figure out another use for it: booze.

The Portuguese sugarcane plantation owners, who had brought knowledge of distillation with them along with their traditional grape distillate *bagaceira*, were likely aided in the development of early sugarcane spirits by local natives. Indigenous Carib tribes, among the first people to work the Portuguese sugar mills, were already known for drinking fermented beverages made from many native plants, including potatoes and cassava, and this knowledge was quickly translated to sugarcane.

Brazil's first sugarcane plantation and, subsequently, the first distillery for Brazil's great sugarcane spirit, cachaça—was established in the early 1500s, on the coast south of São Paulo. The first documented report of a cane distillate in the newly colonized Americas was written from there in 1532 by Portuguese general and governor Tomé de Souza in Brazil, who wrote of plantation slaves drinking a raw-cane spirit they called *cachaço,* the name that in time became *cachaça*. At that time, and for a long time thereafter, the new sugarcane spirit was consumed exclusively by slaves while rich people drank wine and European spirits. But the spirit grew in popularity nonetheless, and steadily made its way inland from the coasts, with each new settlement establishing its farm, its sugar mill, and its distillery together. (When I visited the old water-powered mill of Engenho do Diquinho in the Brazilian state of Paraná, owner Marisa Leal had some paintings depicting the town's history, including one of her father— who'd run the distillery previously—that was captioned "Where the cane mills, the pot distills.")

When the Portuguese overtook the rest of what is now Brazil from the Dutch in 1640, the Dutch fled north and carried sugar-distillation methodologies with them to Guyana and then onward to Barbados and the Caribbean, where they used the knowledge to make spirits from that formerly bothersome by-product of sugar production: molasses. No one really knows when—or where—the very first drops of what we now call rum were produced. But leaving aside the early records of cachaça production (and no proud Brazilian calls their national spirit "rum" anyway!), it's generally accepted that rumlike sugarcane distillates originated in Barbados, with canes and stills supplied by the Dutch. Within just a few decades of colonization, Barbados became Britain's richest colony due to the people's capitalization on the sugar trade and the rum that came with it, and distilleries began to pop up all over Latin America as plantations recognized a new, profitable use for molasses.

Up to that point, molasses had always been a major problem for sugar producers. Sticky, heavy, and not particularly delicious, it wasn't something many local people wanted to eat, and certainly it wasn't worth the trouble to ship back to Europe. Many sugar mills would simply throw it away in the ocean or try to turn it into livestock feed. And the mills had quite a lot of the sticky mess to get rid of—they produced about one pound of molasses for every two pounds of granulated sugar. Inevitably, a lot of molasses ended up sitting around in large vats, where, as with everything else in the equatorial heat and rain and humidity, it would often ferment. Slaves, natives, and colonists alike had taken to drinking the resulting mildly alcoholic liquid to ease their minds; imported wines and beers were far too expensive, but this sugar-water beer dimmed the senses just enough.

When inspiration struck to distill this fermented beverage into a strong spirit, the resulting liquor took off. By the mid-seventeenth century, rums from the then-English colony of Barbados were the most coveted. But, they weren't yet called by the name *rum*; rather, these spirits were known by rum's first name: *kill-devil*. Rum, the later nom de plume for the spirit, is very likely the result of different languages and cultures coming together, and likely came from the word *rumbullion*, a portmanteau of the Old English word *rum*, meaning "good," and the French *bouillon*, meaning a strong, hot drink—which also happens to carry the synonyms of "rebellion," "uproar," and "turmoil." Summed up: rum is a good sort of rebellion. Sounds excellent to me!

Although the English may have found it to be "good" in the sense that it got the job done alcoholically, in the beginning, not everyone was especially fond of the new spirit's taste. But by the end of the seventeenth century, rum had started to take on more of a refined taste, and what had begun as a harsh fire-water birthed a bustling industry that began to make sugar-plantation owners all the wealthier. The spirit soon became a staple of the open seas, with sailors from every nation drinking their daily dram and then some, to drunken delight.

Everything was going swimmingly—for the conquerors, anyway—with sugar and rum production clipping along. Then, in the nineteenth century, two very important things happened almost simultaneously: the popularization of sugar beets in Europe and the abolition of slavery by the British Empire.

The first of these large changes was due in large part to aggressive advocacy by that enthusiastic nationalist, Napoleon, who was always looking for ways to consolidate imperial power back at home. To him, the sugar beet was the agricultural answer to a thorny problem of international dependency: produce sugar with beets—which European farmers were able to grow easily and cheaply in European soil—and you can stop relying on sugar that must be imported from your colonies abroad. This became especially pressing after the Haitian Revolution left France bereft of that lucrative colony in 1804.

As economic reliance on the colonies and cheap equatorial labor dropped, abolitionist movements gained in power, and vice versa; and in 1833, the British Empire formally abolished slavery, setting the precedent for subsequent decrees in France and the United States. Hundreds of sugarcane plantations—and rum distilleries—closed as the beet-sugar industry boomed and sugarcane production, which now had to be paid for (imagine!), became more and more

The growth of white wispy flowers shows that the sugarcane is ready for harvest. Rhum J.M, Le Macouba, Martinique.

expensive. Sugar production began to migrate out of the West Indies and back to Asia, where much of the industry remains today.

And just when it was needed most, a major technological development arose that almost single-handedly saved the rum industry by making distillation itself far cheaper, counterbalancing the loss of cheap labor due to abolition: the column still. An almost entirely mechanized mode of distillation, which required very little human monitoring, this allowed distillation to be accomplished without the effort it had always demanded—which meant that (at least some of) the money that now had to be spent on farm laborers to grow and harvest sugarcane could be recouped later down the line. (Not long thereafter, when the Industrial Revolution got into full swing, farm equipment and the harvesting process moved toward mechanization, too, which further reduced the need for human labor.) Rum was saved and began to develop the style by which most of the world best knows it today: lighter, smoother, and many times distilled.

Around the same time as these developments, the Spanish, following a string of wars that liberated many of their South American territories, placed a new emphasis on building up their early sugarcane-haven colonies of Cuba and Puerto Rico. They decided it would be best to keep slavery around for a while in those places to gain a competitive edge while they licked their wounds from losing their stronghold in South America. Slavery (which wouldn't be abolished in Puerto Rico until 1873, or in Cuba until 1886) was back in business. A new agricultural class emigrating from other European countries purchased slaves in large numbers and moved to the Spanish colonies, and Spain overtook the role of the world's king of sugarcane.

The Spanish began to produce their own style of rum on a worldwide commercial scale. This began in Cuba—where a stint of British naval occupation in Havana in the mid-eighteenth century had first gotten rum and rum production going—and then spread to Puerto Rico via Cuban emigrés. Dubbed *ron ligero* or "light rum," this was rum in the modern, continuous-stilled style, fashioned for the European tastes of the Spanish nobility. Sweet, age-mellowed, and refined in palate—while still strong enough to get you good and drunk—this new Spanish style of rum quickly gained popularity and forever changed the worldwide perception of what rum should be. Today, Spanish-style rum is the most popular style in the world; Bacardi, which manufactures rum of this style, is arguably the most recognizable spirits brand worldwide.

SOY CANTINERO

Of all the places in Latin America that I visited, Cuba, and Havana in particular, is really the only one that has a cocktail-making culture built into its history. So many classic drinks hail from there; the Mojito and the daiquiri to name two. During Prohibition, making drinks there was somewhat as it is now: a fantastic way to make money, meet interesting people, and be involved in a global cultural interchange. There was a vibrant culture of *cantineros*—bartenders and spirits enthusiasts who often served as the ambassadors of Cuban culture to the rest of the jet-setting world.

After the country's communist revolution of the 1950s, all that changed. Fidel Castro was ideologically against nightlife, and he shut down just about every one of the country's classic bars. Only a few of the old *cantineros* remained working, while many fled afar. But with time, the lift of the U.S. embargo and the re-encouragement of the country's hotel economy—bringing tips from foreign visitors—recent years have begun to see the resurgence of Cuba's *cantinero* culture.

"Bartending is an aspirational career here in Cuba again," Cuban-born *Maestro Cantinero* (master bartender) Julio Cabrera told me as we sat outside the famous El Floridita bar. Julio escaped communism by moving to Miami with a life built on bartending. "Before the revolution, if you were a doctor or lawyer or engineer, you made a lot of money," he explained. "But that all changed. I was educated as an engineer, and I thought to myself, Why should I work like this for $20 a day, when I could become a bartender and make the same amount in tips in two hours? I remember my first shift: I made $80 in tips. It blew my mind." That mentality has spread in Cuba, too, Cabrera said. "Now, you see a lot of bartenders who used to be doctors."

Organizations in Cuba work to keep the *cantinero* distinction relevant. While there, I visited the club of the *Asociación de Cantineros de Cuba*, where I got to see the passion that these (mostly) men have for their jobs and their craft. The storied past of the Cuban *cantinero* was palpable there. It was a unique glimpse at Latin American history and historical preservation, viewed through the lens of classic cocktail culture by an organization that upholds that culture as a point of national pride.

A crucial encourager of the Cuban rum boom was the growing thirst of its also-booming neighbor, the United States. With the end of the Spanish-American War in 1898, Cuba became a protectorate of the United States, tourism to the island took off, and *ron ligero*—and the growing variety of delicious cocktails you could make from it—became a hot commodity stateside. Some of the first bars in the Americas popped up in Havana to serve the rich and famous visitors vacationing there, and the era of the cocktail was ushered in.

When Prohibition hit in the United States, it didn't halt light rum's popularity one bit; on the contrary, it spurred it on even harder, as the trip to Cuba from the south of Florida was just a quick jaunt away. After Prohibition was lifted, Havana's reputation for a good time persisted, and cocktail bars—owned by locals and American expatriates alike—continued to flourish there. Famous writers such as Ernest Hemingway gave worldwide notoriety to Cuban rum, Cuban cocktails, and the classy Havana bars where they originated.

Nowadays it's easy to forget, in light of the popularity that Spanish-style rum has achieved, that sugarcane spirits are made in many other styles as well. As we'll learn, there's a vast array of different styles out there—from grassy, funky Brazilian cachaça to full-bodied, unctuous Jamaican rums. Unfortunately for this wonderful diversity of flavor, the world's largest rum producers, by and large, have committed themselves to making rum according to an exaggerated version of the *ron ligero* model: light, highly refined, and without most of the original characteristics of the natural sugarcane from which it is produced—basically a sugarcane vodka. But *rum itself*, the original free spirit, in fact represents nuance and diversity on a global scale, a spirit as stylistically varied as the many places it hails from.

Nicolay Mesa Chavez famed *cantinero* of El Floridita, bartends at the club Cantineros de Cuba, Havana, Cuba.

Fieldworkers maneuver a cane harvester through a field, Nueva Paz, Cuba.

THE REAL COST OF SUGARCANE

No one who researches the history and production of sugar and rum can remain ignorant of the tragedy and human sacrifice attached to it. Almost as horrific, however, are the many ways that sacrifice continues today. Diseases, dehydration, and exhaustion are especially dangerous under the conditions of cane harvesting, and the industry generally provides little money to deal with the illnesses that can result.

As the twenty-first century passed into its second decade, chronic kidney disease (CKD) became the second-deadliest killer in Central America. CKD, a disease caused by heat, stress, and dehydration— exactly the working conditions of most sugarcane fields (especially hand-harvested ones)—is unsurprisingly rampant among the sugar farmers. Sugar workers' shifts can last many hours, as they are generally paid according to what they reap, rather than how long they've been there. Oftentimes, no food or water is supplied to them, let alone shade or rest.

I have to say that in my travels, I didn't see such conditions. In fact, in most of the fields I visited, the opposite was the case. (In Cuba, perhaps in keeping with the country's communist ethos, the cane field I visited had a little wooden shed, pulled behind a tractor, with its own friendly chef who served the workers sweet treats and sweet coffee.) But the invisibility of the problem elsewhere is one of rum's most sinister aspects, and in recent years, the news has broken that many people in this industry are quite literally working themselves to death.

The rum industry has the ability to change this, of course. Working conditions need to be transparent, not only for those who work in distilleries but also for those working in the sugar refineries supplying distilleries with molasses. And as part of this transparency, we, the consumers, should expect to pay a higher price for safe working conditions. After all, rum isn't cheap because it's easy to produce; it's cheap because of the cheapness of the labor that goes into it—an expectation that goes back to the days of slavery.

For an example of the way things can be done, look at the Caribbean island of Martinique. Everyone in Martinique, from sugarcane farmers to master blenders to distillery owners, enjoys the same legal protection as their counterparts in France (because, well, Martinique *is* France). That means they get protection under strict labor laws, a higher minimum wage, a thirty-five-hour workweek, free healthcare, paid vacation time, and so on. Because of this, Martinique's rhum agricole is more expensive to make and ends up being a few dollars more expensive to buy, but it's a great product, and one you can feel good about buying, too.

PRODUCTION

Not only is sugarcane inherently sweet and truly a dream plant for fermenting and distilling but, being part of the grass family, it also grows rapidly (up to an inch a day!), densely, and very high—upward of twenty feet in height, in nine to eighteen months—making it a fantastic maximum-yield crop. (The cane also grows through multiple seasons before replanting is necessary.) Today there are around fifteen thousand different subspecies, many of which have been bred to ward off disease and infection. Rum producers select from a much more limited range of varietals and will often mix and match types to obtain certain desired characteristics.

Unlike agaves, which can survive in the most arid of landscapes, sugarcane needs a lot of water to keep its sacchariferous cells hydrated. If you want the best concentration of sugar in the cane, you have to cut it at just the right time in its growth, shortly after it flowers. Harvesting can be accomplished by hand or by machine, but while machine harvesting is much less labor-intensive, it's massively expensive (with machines costing upward of $2 million) and can only be done properly when the ground is flat. Machine harvesters, truly awesome machines straight out of *Transformers*, inch down sugarcane fields with wild corkscrew pistons like the tusks of a mechanical woolly mammoth spiralling through the canes, cutting them from the ground and stripping them of their leaves. Wherever these machines go, you see hundreds of birds following in their wake, snapping up the bugs that they toss loose from the cane.

Harvesting sugarcane by hand, however, has to be one of the world's most arduous jobs. Even under the best conditions, it's sweaty and oppressive work, reserved for the bottom of the workforce totem pole. Workers use sharp machetes and hack through the hard stalks of the bamboo-like canes to detach them from the leafy "cane trash"; stack and then carry loads of cut canes through scorching-hot fields; and finally load them onto donkeys or into wheelbarrows or trucks. That being said, just about every person I met who did this job showed a strong sense of pride in what he was doing.

The cane, like corn, produces large, leafy blades that dry out and droop as the plant grows. The leaves contain zero usable sugar and provide a safe haven for bugs, snakes, and other creepy-crawly things, while creating a dense tangle for the harvester to hack his way through. Because of this, when sugarcane is harvested by hand, the farmers tend to burn the fields first, to clear away as much of this extraneous matter and chase away as many of these troublesome critters as possible. Field burning doesn't affect the cane's ability to regrow, remarkably, but some farmers believe that it does change the flavor of the juice (and ultimately its distillate) down the line. Not surprisingly, it also leads to all kinds of environmental problems and human health maladies, so some countries—such as Brazil, since 2011—have outlawed the practice of burning altogether. In other countries, though, it's still done regularly. In Jamaica, on my way to visit Hampden Estate, I drove past a field fully ablaze, with seemingly no one in sight to tend to it. For Americans raised on news of devastating forest fires in the West, it was a frightful and chaotic sight to behold—though clearly nothing out of the ordinary for the others passing by.

After harvest, the canes are then cut, crushed, and pressed or pounded, separating the juice (called *guarapo* in Spanish-speaking countries, or *jus* in French) from the crunchy fibers (also called *bagasso* or *bagasse*). This part of the process can be done in ancient water mills as I saw in Brazil, by mills driven by donkeys or oxen as I saw in Haiti and Mexico, or by electric or gas motor; many producers use roller mills, in which the sliced-and-diced cane is crushed with water.

THE DIVERSE SPIRIT OF BRAZIL

"Brazil is a melting pot, with a huge frontier. We neighbor with just about every other South American country, and our own population contains all the world's ethnicities. Despite what people think sometimes, we are a happy and peaceful people, of thousands of different types—and that's what cachaça is too."—Thyrso Camargo, Yaguara Cachaça

Brazil is not only the world's fifth-largest country. It's also a country extremely diverse in terms of climate and biodiversity, containing rain forests and mountains, coastlines and deserts. Human diversity is equally impressive. Brazil's population is extraordinarily ethnically diverse, and the country is home to huge populations of emigrants from elsewhere. Local languages, religions, cuisines, and cultures vary widely from one part of the country to another, and these characteristics combine in new and fascinating ways all the time.

The national spirit of such a vast, diverse country should be vast and diverse itself; and Brazilian cachaça is exactly that. As Novo Fogo's master distiller, Dr. Agenor Maccari, put it, "We have not cachaça, but cachaças." Literally tens of thousands of different cachaças are made in Brazil—out of sugarcane, and aged in woods, that grow practically everywhere in the country—and their variability is enormous. Some cachaças come from thousands of feet above sea level, where the sugarcane grows alongside grapes; some cachaças are made right next to the sea, deep in the jungle, or from rocky desert areas. All of these environments, and the people who inhabit them, are capable of bringing out different qualities from cane and barrel alike. Brazil has to maintain three separate official DOs, with the emphasis for each tending to fall on the end product, rather than the process used to achieve it. As the great cachaceiro Mauricio Maia explained it to me while we sipped some pinga in a roadside boteco (Brazil's local watering holes, which are sprinkled along roads the whole country over), "The Brazilian regulations don't tell you how you must do, just what you must do. Column or alembic, open or closed fermentation, natural yeast or chemicals—that's all up to you."

Roadside bars, or *botecos*, are everywhere in Brazil. Here, at Gil-Bar, owner Gilson Soares is ready to serve. Morretes, Paraná, Brazil.

From here, the sugarcane juice can then follow a few different paths to fermentation and, ultimately, to being distilled into rum. It can be refined into sugar first, after which the by-product of that refinement, molasses, is what enters the fermentation process. It also can be made into cane syrup or cane honey, which is simply concentrated cane juice, produced after the initial evaporation stage of sugar refining. (In my Vermonter's view, this is like boiling down maple sap to make syrup, and it's done for the same reasons: it gives the product a longer shelf life and concentrates the sweetness so that it won't ferment.) Or, in the most straightforward route, the sugarcane juice can immediately enter fermentation on its own.

Excluding French-style rhums (especially those made in the six or seven hundred distilleries in Haiti) and all of the cachaça in Brazil, about 90 percent of all rum made in Latin America is made from fermenting blackstrap molasses. With the sugar-refining process that ultimately gives us molasses, the juice from the cane goes through concentration and crystallization. This is achieved by evaporating the water from the juice, after which we end up with crystallized sugar and tarlike molasses. Generally the juice goes through multiple separate boilings to extract all of the sugar crystals, and in each boiling, the molasses becomes darker, thicker, and more bitter; the molasses left over after the last boiling is "blackstrap" molasses, a very thick, flavorful syrup that's still rich enough in sugars for fermentation but simply too much of a hassle (and therefore prohibitively expensive) to boil again. With all this fire, heavy machinery, and boiling sugar around, you can bet that sugar refineries tend to be crazy, extremely difficult-to-keep-clean places. When I was in Cuba, I got to explore one in a massive, old warehouse that had to have been six stories high, full of *Wizard of Oz*–like flames bursting from furnaces and gusts of steam hissing out at random intervals. (I'd recommend checking it out yourself, but that might be kind of a tall order; like many things in government-run Cuba, the giant, noisy, steam-belching factory was supposed to be secret.)

Rum made directly from sugarcane juice or syrup is commonly referred to as *rhum agricole*, a French term meaning "agricultural rum." As the name implies, this is meant to be a smaller, more farm-to-table type of rum, made not from the by-product of an industrial process on a great big plantation but from the juice of the plant itself. The process is as simple and direct as possible: the sugarcane is crushed, water is sometimes added, and fermentation begins.

RHUM AGRICOLE AND RHUM INDUSTRIEL

Karine Lassalle from Rhum J.M described rhum agricole to me as "just as elegant and complex as our people." And it is indeed French. Unlike other nations, whose rum functioned primarily as a by-product of the sugar industry, the French actively tried to suit European palates with their product and applied the refinement techniques they'd perfected with calvados, cognac, and armagnac to their rhums.

In contrast to the reckless abandon of most other rums, rhum agricole is highly legislated. Among other things, this allows for an oh-so-French delineation between "rhum agricole" (rums made in traditional French style) and "rhum industriel" (all those other kinds of rum out there). This legislation is accomplished via Appellations d'Origine Contrôlée (AOC), the French equivalent of Denominations of Origin, which lay down the rules regarding the production of a number of French agricultural products.

One of rhum agricole's legally recognized territories, the French Caribbean island of Martinique, which makes some of the best rhum agricole in the world, established its own additional AOC in 1996. This set of specifications regulates matters such as acceptable plantation yields (not too much, now!), additives (none!), sugarcane types (twenty), fermentation time (only up to seventy-two hours), and distillation methods (column). It also places no requirements on aging, which makes Martinique's rhum agricole the world's only AOC-regulated white spirit. Though Martinique contributes less than 1 percent of the world's rum, it's well aware that most of the other 99 percent probably isn't a fraction as delicious—and they credit their AOC with the distinction. "It's the Champagne of rum," said Ben Jones of SPIRIBAM, a distributor and marketer of fine Caribbean rums. "That's what the AOC has given the category."

Marisa Leal of Engenho do Diquino presses her hand-cut cane using a water-powered wheel. Morretes, Paraná, Brazil.

CACHAÇA'S "INFORMAL SECTOR"

Today, cachaça is officially the fourth most-consumed distilled beverage in the world, with around five thousand unique brands producing somewhere in the vicinity of a billion liters of cachaça every year. This may sound like a lot, but by many estimates, those five thousand official brands only account for about 15 percent of the cachaça actually produced in Brazil. The other 85 percent, made by distilleries operating without legal recognition, is hidden—in plain sight. (Driving around Brazil, it's not hard to find these small stills and see what each particular family's stuff is made of; it's actually the perfect way to spend a day.)

Because of this, cachaça may well be the most-consumed distilled beverage in the world: by some estimates, up to 98 percent of all cachaça is consumed within Brazil. As a result, the extent of most non-Brazilians' knowledge of the spirit revolves around the famous cocktail that incorporates it, the Caipirinha—a delicious claim to fame, to be sure, but by no means all there is.

So why is so much cachaça kept off the books? The main answer, as usual, is money. Brazil's taxes on its registered distillates are, for lack of a better word, outrageous. They reach from 70 percent to as high as 82 percent, regardless of whether the producer is a global corporation with exports to fifty countries, or a woman with a sugar press rigged up to a water wheel. Throw in the nation's insatiable appetite for cachaça, and the unbelievable fact that Brazil's Ministry of Agriculture—the department that oversees cachaça-making on national, state, and city levels—has only twenty-seven people working to monitor the country's spirits, wine, beer, and soda (let me say that again: twenty-seven people for all of Brazil!), and you have the makings of one hell of a black market.

In Brazil, distillers also make their national spirit out of fermented fresh sugarcane juice. They call it *cachaça*, after the Portuguese word for the foam that rises from the boiling juice. (It's also known by many wonderful provincial names, including *pinga* [it drips], *malvada* [she-devil], *água-benta* [blessed water], and *assovio-de-cobra* [snake's whistle].) Originally cachaça was made from straight sugarcane juice simply because that was what Brazilian sugarcane producers had the most of. Brazil had, and still has, the most abundant lands in the world for growing sugarcane, so distillers had more than enough juice to make both sugar and cachaça. In the mid-1960s, using only fresh juice was made a legal requirement for cachaça distillation, and it has remained one ever since.

With both rhum agricole and cachaça, then, fermentation begins immediately after the juice is pressed from the sugarcane. Because there aren't any other refining steps in between plant and spirit, it is arguably with these types of rum that we get the clearest window into the flavors and terroir of sugarcane: drinking them is like biting right into the sugarcane itself.

With rums made from cane syrup and molasses, on the other hand— that is, all other kinds of rum—some other things need to be done first. Molasses and syrup don't generally have enough water content (that is, their sugar concentration is too high) to create a consistently ideal environment for fermentation—which in other contexts is a good thing, since it's what gives them their longer shelf life. With most types of sugarcane distillate, yeast is added to the mix to jumpstart (and control) fermentation, but in some cases, airborne yeast is allowed to start the fermentation process on its own. Some rums are fermented for only short periods in order to avoid high esters—the deeper, funkier flavors that fermentation imparts. Some traditionally bold, rich rums, on the other hand, like those from Jamaica, incorporate longer fermentation times in order to intensify these flavors.

In any case, the fermenting brew—which can smell anywhere from delicious to unctuous, often like apples or bananas—is referred to as *must*, *mosto*, or *vin*, depending on the language of the producer. After its fermentation period, the brew is ready to distill.

A NOTE ON CLAIRIN . . . AND SOME OTHER LESSER-KNOWN SUGARCANE AGUARDIENTES

Today, in all the Caribbean, only a few dozen legally recognized distilleries are producing rum—a massive drop from rum's heyday. So when I visited Haiti to learn about their local sugarcane aguardiente, clairin, I was utterly blown away to learn that the country has more than six hundred distilleries still operating. As with the many legally unrecognized cachaças in Brazil, or legally unrecognized mezcals in Oaxaca, these distilleries are often tiny, semi-clandestine operations that work in a very rudimentary manner. They make their spirit from hand-harvested cane juice, some using French Creole-style stills and others using some of the craziest welded-stacks-of-metal stills I've ever seen. The stuff is just as beautiful as its country, and it is absolutely delicious.

Clairin is one of many such "hidden" sugarcane spirits out there in Latin America: aguardientes whose lack of their own DO, or nonconformity with existing ones, has led them to be unduly ignored by the rest of the world. Luckily in the case of clairin, Luca Gargano, an Italian rum specialist and owner of global distributor Velier, elected to introduce the world to this beautiful stuff. But a lot of other great sugarcane aguardientes are also out there—made from both fresh juice and molasses, and almost never aged—hailing from Oaxaca (Hello, Paranubes!), Michoacan (Check out charanda, a DO-protected Mexican sugarcane spirit), Guatemala, Peru . . . the list goes on and on. If you're traveling in a lush tropical land, sugarcane likely grows there, and an interesting local spirit may be right under your nose.

Wooden fermentation vats at Hampden Estate, a distillery famous for its highly funky rum. Falmouth, Jamaica.

DUNDER STYLE

We in the cocktail industry have a thing for intense flavor, for complex contrasts of sensation, for high esters—in a word, for funk. And nothing screams funk in rum like some of the special-batch pot-stilled rums they make in Jamaica under the name "Dunder style."

Dunder-style rum—which, despite how highly it's coveted, accounts for only 2 percent of Jamaica's total rum production—is fermented much like sourdough bread: one uses a fermentation "starter" to jumpstart each next batch. In this case, however, the starter is a "dunder pit." Often this is a literal pit, filled with molasses, water, cane vinegar . . . and other stuff.

All sorts of fables exist, of people throwing horrible things into these pits—human feces and animal carcasses among them—originally (as the story runs) to keep slaves from drinking the soon-to-be-distilled brew, and later for the additional flavor and aid to fermentation that they imparted. In reality, the nastiest thing that goes into a dunder pit is just the harsh, semi-toxic stillage by-product that we call vinasse: a highly acidic sludge left over after distillation that retains all sorts of interesting flavors and aromas.

The result is funky—truly the highest-ester rums in the world. As a benchmark, most white rums out there being poured by your local bartender have ester counts of less than 50 grams per hectoliter of absolute alcohol (g/hL). Jamaica's high-ester rums generally max out at 500 g/hL, with a legal maximum of 1,600 g/hL! While visiting the idyllic Hampden Estate, I tasted rums with an ester count of nearly 2,000 g/hL, and I was told that the count can go up as high as 7,000! Rums this intensely flavorful are generally used for nondrinking purposes, as concentrates to flavor ice cream or to scent perfumes. I personally love the stuff (the funkier the better!), so I brought some home for select sipping. We even use Hampden Estate's Rum Fire in dasher bottles at Leyenda to bring just a little nuance to a drink in need.

SPICE IT UP

Even the broad, lawless category of rum eventually runs up against one limit. Many rum enthusiasts exclude spiced rum from the list of so-called real rums. Before I traveled in the Caribbean, I was certainly of this camp myself; I thought of spiced rum as an overly sweet, low-proof syrup, closer to a spiced liqueur than to a rum. Hangover in a bottle? No thanks.

Now, having visited a few of the places where spiced rum originated and remains popular—particularly St. Lucia and Haiti, both of which are known for their spiced elixirs—I'm still not a huge fan of the stuff in terms of taste, but I can no longer dispute its authenticity. Spiced rum goes back practically as far as rum itself in the Caribbean, where it got its start as a medicinal drink; it was a way of preserving herbs and spices for use in remedies for everything from headache to heartbreak.

Spiced rum is generally made with higher-proof spirits, which take better to infusions. In St. Lucia, it's still popular to make and drink your own; St. Lucia Distillers makes a whole brand of unaged high-proof rum meant for use in local tinctures, and it seems like practically every shop and household there has its own recipe. After my visit to St. Lucia, I ended up thinking of spiced rum as a cocktail in and of itself, and I tried making a few different drinks based around it. My preference is for unsweetened spiced rums, but try making an infusion yourself with different spices and then mix up a simple daiquiri from it. The results can be delicious and wonderfully varied.

Today, we see both pot and column stills of just about every shape and size used in rum creation. Some specialized types of stills are also commonly used, including the double-retort pot still used to make some English-style rums, and the "Creole column" used to make rhum agricole, which incorporates bell-shaped plates inside the column to control the way the rising steam interacts with the falling liquid ferment. The vast majority of rums made around the world incorporate both pot- and column-stilling technology, for flavor, cost-efficiency, and consistency.

Sugarcane spirits often undergo aging after distillation. In fact, aging in barrels (both intentionally and unintentionally) has been an inextricable part of rum from the very beginning, when the spirit was shipped in barrels across the ocean from the Americas to Europe, and when sailors (and pirates!) brought it along with them on long overseas voyages. The added benefit to this long-term storage in barrels, as sailors and merchants quickly discovered, was that it turned a blazing-hot, hardly palatable white spirit into something very different and, in fact, quite appetizing.

As a result, most rums (especially those exported from their countries of origin) continue to be aged today as part of their identities, and a real mastery can be found among the men and women who watch the barrels over years of aging and blend their contents for maximum consistency.

Aging can be done in different ways, using different woods. As with so many spirits, old American whiskey barrels tend to be used a lot because they're so readily available; in French-style rhums, we see a lot of European oak used. Cachaça introduces a *ton* of other woods.

The simplest way to do the aging is the old standby practice of one barrel at a time, with larger or smaller barrels being used to impart different degrees of woodiness to the spirit. Keep in mind, however, that in the hot tropics, aging happens at a rate sometimes three times faster than in cooler climates, so much more of each barrel is lost to the angels. The emptier the barrel, the more warm air will be in there and the faster the remaining spirit will evaporate; so spirit makers in the tropics have found ways to keep their barrels full. The solera aging process, for example, involves moving small parts of white rum from younger barrels to older and older barrels, resulting in an aged rum that contains traces of spirit as old as the solera itself. In Martinique and Jamaica, they employ an *oeillage* aging process in which, each year to the day,

Copper column stills at Rhum J.M, Le Macouba, Martinique.

they consolidate all of their partially evaporated barrels, refilling the resulting empties with raw spirit to start the process over.

In Cuba, the art of blending and aging has been elevated to the level of a guiding principle in its rum making. When I visited Havana Club, Asbel Morales explained their elaborate process: rather than blending and continuously aging one batch of rum for one period of time, they create blends using different vintages of aged rum as their raw materials, then age and reblend them, sometimes through many separate processes. This allows them to create intricate, sometimes extremely long-aged rums that retain the flavors and aromas of many different ages, rather than allowing those subtleties to be dominated by the wood characteristics that the same length of time spent in a single barrel would impart.

Besides being unduly fetishized, as they are with all spirits nowadays, age statements with rum can create serious confusion when it comes to classifying the stuff. This goes back to the lawlessness of the spirit as a whole: many rum-producing countries, though they may have strict laws defining the use of age statements on their rum labels, don't necessarily monitor the enforcement of them, and each country may have different laws stating what its age statements even mean. This, along with the fact that the majority of rums are blended, leads to a lot of label ambiguity. Some producers end up using age statements to signify the youngest of the rums that are blended in a bottle's contents (as in, no rum in that blend came from a barrel younger than the number mentioned); others use them to signify the oldest-aged rum included (essentially the opposite: the youngest rum could be right off the still, while the number on the label could account for a minimal percentage of what's in the bottle); still others take the average age of all the rums in the mix, and identify the blend by that number. Throw in the further consideration that the aging process happens very differently in the many climates where rum is made, and age statements on rum labels start to look pretty meaningless.

Indeed, this kind of anarchy makes *any* classification of rum a daunting task. Unlike any of the other spirits in this book, rum can legally be made anywhere in the world, and is produced in upward of sixty countries; and if you've ever had a look at international politics, it will come as no surprise that none of the countries seem to be able to agree on terms. Consequently, just as a label saying that a rum is fifteen or twenty years old tells us nothing about how much of what's in the bottle is actually that old, or what that age implies for its flavor, a label that describes a rum as "dark," or "gold," or "white" may well be telling us nothing about that spirit other than how much caramel coloring has been added to it.

This is not to say that there aren't rum-classification systems out there that have made some headway. The Gargano system—created in 2015 by two of the greatest modern minds in rum, Luca Gargano of spirits distributor Velier and Richard Seale of Foursquare Distillery in Barbados—is the most recent, and to many, the most successful attempt at rum classification. It classifies rum by blend and method of production, contrasting traditional pot-stilled rums with those made in more modern multiple-column-still plants, and blended rums with single-distillery rums. Sensible as this system is, though, I agree with the critics who argue that it tends to group rums, often unfairly, into "good" and "bad" on the basis of their distilling technique, landing single-distillery, pot-stilled rums on the good side and blended column-stilled rums on the bad.

> "If you just classify based on technicalities, you lose the romanticism and history of what rum is."
>
> —MARGARET MONPLAISIR, ST. LUCIA DISTILLERS

Cultural origins, to me, are essential to rum classification and the rum-classification type I find most useful is probably the one rum-drinkers have been using the longest: a grouping of style by geographical and historical origin makes sense. Following this basic structure, we get a division of rum into the categories of English style (both column- and pot-distilled from molasses, rich and flavorful), Jamaican style (an offshoot of the English, mostly pot-distilled from molasses, heavy and unctuous), Spanish style (column-distilled from molasses, light in flavor), and French/Brazilian style (both column- and pot-distilled from fresh sugarcane juice, funky and grassy). I am very much aware of the unfairness of this last grouping, on its surface: Brazilian spirits production is not at all French in origin, cachaça is very much its own thing and pre-dates the other styles of rum, et cetera. But this being a categorization based on style, it makes sense to think of cachaça as similar to rhums produced in the French style.

THE WONDERFUL VARIETY OF BRAZILIAN WOODS

I'm always saying unaged spirits tend to be the spirits for me, but that opinion goes right out the window when it comes to cachaça and the many indigenous woods that Brazilians use to age their national spirit.

When sugarcane spirits were first produced in Brazil, any spirit that wasn't imbibed immediately was aged in wood. In lush, heavily forested Brazil, it was always much easier to get hold of native wood for barrels than clay, steel, or glass for storage containers. And since these neutral materials became widely available there only later, it can be argued that unaged cachaça is the modern-day exception to the rule. (Even today, only about 10 percent of cachaça is unaged.)

As cachaça took hold, it began to be barrel-aged in local woods as a matter of course. Today, about 30 percent of all cachaça is aged in more than thirty different types of Brazilian woods, each with its own unique flavor and aromatic profiles: from the strong cinnamon-nut-crunchiness of *amburana* to the brisk, earthy astringency of *balsamo*.

Unfortunately, many areas in Brazil have been heavily deforested, and some of the woods commonly used in barrel-making are now being protected as they draw perilously close to extinction. Recognizing the traditional importance of these woods, some of the more scrupulous cachaça producers are even taking an active role in conservation and reforestation: Novo Fogo, for instance, is working with an arborist to locate ancient trees in the Atlantic Forest, collect seeds from them, and reforest them elsewhere. The forest has lost more than 85 percent of its original area, and many of its trees and animals are endangered; I was thrilled to join in the attempt to reverse that.

One of the many cavernous, cathedral-like aging rooms of Rhum Clément, Le François, Martinique.

Now, granted, rums from one area can vary wildly in flavor, just as similarly produced rums from very different areas can taste very similar. It can also be argued that the national classification is antiquated and even bigoted, in that it defines rum—a spirit of incredible racial and cultural complexity—primarily according to its oppressive European colonial beginnings. As horrific as these nations' histories often were, the combining of cultures within them tends to make some sense of the identities of the rums that they produced and continue to make. These spirits are truthful expressions: their styles reflect both the positive and negative aspects of their history.

Rum, rhum, cachaça, aguardiente—sugarcane spirits are truly a diverse creation, a mixture emblematic of so much of Latin America. Trying to lock down definitions and categories for these incredible spirits is difficult at best, and at worst pointless; among all the world's spirit types, these spirits encapsulate just how vast and various humanity can be. The countries they hail from are more than all-inclusive resorts and carefree havens for sunburns and piña coladas on the beach; very often their histories include some of the cruelest periods in the life of our species, and some of its most impressive triumphs over that cruelty. But from revolutions and wars to peace and plenty, from poverty to wealth, from sorrow to celebration, sugarcane spirits remain the drinkable manifestation of diversity.

RUM STYLES

FRENCH STYLE The French opted to use the fresh sugarcane juice itself for their spirits. Distilled generally in column stills, but also in pot stills, this grassy liquid is generally known as rhum agricole.

BRAZILIAN CACHAÇA Like the French, the Brazilians opted to make their rum out of fermented sugarcane juice rather than molasses. This is done in column and pot stills; the distillate must legally be bottled between 38 percent and 48 percent, whereas its cousin rhum agricole can boast proofs upward of 110.

ENGLISH STYLE The English were first to start making their sugar by-products into rum, this style of rum, made from molasses or demerara sugar (aka turbinado sugar, a type of partially refined sugar from Guyana), is the oldest traditional style. It tends to be heavy-bodied and rich, with lots of flavor nuances and funk. Traditionally made with pot stills, later blended from pot- and column-stilled products, and now increasingly made with column stills, this rum can be aged or unaged; the real distinction of an English-style rum is its blend of different stills and techniques. In its past, this was a puritan, high-proof style, but it's frequently now made a little lighter and less intense.

JAMAICAN STYLE An offshoot of the English style known for its high esters, this rum is made from molasses, often with slow methods of fermentation for more funk. A characteristic example of this is the so-called Dunder style, while others are lighter. Both column and pot stills are used and blended in English style.

SPANISH STYLE A generally more efficient molasses-based spirit, this style is refined, light, and less funky. Column-stilled, charcoal-filtered, and barrel-aged, Spanish-style rum is the type best known to Americans since Prohibition, and increasingly emulated around the world. The majority of big rum brands nowadays mimic this *ron ligero* style, in many cases only achieving a vodka-like sugar distillate with little flavor.

A field worker slices a stalk of sugarcane for a midday snack. Nueva Paz, Cuba

MOJITO

8 to 10 mint leaves

¾ oz Simple Syrup
(see page 243)

¾ oz lime juice

2 oz Havana Club 3 Rum
(or Banks Rum or
Plantation Three Stars)

1 oz club soda

Mint sprig for garnish

When I was in Havana, I made a point of drinking a Mojito in every bar I went to. (The resulting fresh buzz I had while walking the picturesque city was fantastic!) But perhaps my favorite memory was when I was asked behind the bar at the famed Hotel Nacional to whip some up for a group of visiting *cantineros*. The bar was the favorite of many of the celebrity elite who visited during their heyday; pictures of Ernest Hemingway, Jimmy Carter, Ava Gardner, and more line the walls. It was like stepping back in time to make one of the world's most iconic cocktails.

This drink is some bartenders' worst nightmare, especially when they're busy, but it happens to be my guilty pleasure— beautiful, delicious, and refreshing. If you can't get your hands on some Havana Club, try making it with either Banks or Plantation Three Stars rum.

Muddle the mint leaves and simple syrup in the bottom of a Collins glass. Add the lime juice and rum and fill half the glass with pebbled or crushed ice, being sure to keep the mint neatly on the bottom of the glass. Swizzle the ice lightly with a spoon until the glass gets nice and frosty. Add the club soda and top with fresh ice. Garnish with the mint sprig.

CAIPIRINHA

½ lime, cut into quarters

1 tsp superfine sugar

2 oz Novo Fogo
Silver Cachaça

This is one of those cases in which (outside of Brazil, anyway) the cocktail is better known than the spirit in it. This Latin classic started as a medicine for the Spanish flu, and the original recipe contained cachaça, lime, honey . . . and garlic. At some point, some bright-minded person decided to remove the garlic and replace the honey with sugar, and the rest was a much more delicious history.

You can get a version of this at just about every bar or restaurant. I like to give them a real hard shake to express more of the flavorful oils of the limes.

Add the quartered half-lime and sugar to a cocktail shaker and muddle fiercely. Add ice and the cachaça. Shake hard and pour into a rocks glass. No garnish.

MAI TAI

1 oz Appleton Reserve Jamaican Rum

½ oz Smith & Cross Jamaican Rum

½ oz Clement Rhum VSOP

½ oz Pierre Ferrand Orange Curaçao

½ oz Orgeat Works T'Orgeat Toasted Almond Syrup

¾ oz lime juice

Sugarcane stick for garnish (optional)

Edible orchid for garnish (optional)

Mint sprig for garnish

Lime wheel for garnish

The Mai Tai is one of the most fantastic—yet most bastardized—classic rum tiki drinks. Made famous by the iconic Trader Vic in 1944 (so the story goes) in his eponymous Oakland tiki haven, this drink, whose name means "the best" in Tahitian, can be seen today in bars and beach clubs from Honolulu to Cancún, in various forms far from the original concoction.

One thing's for sure: this recipe needs Jamaican rum. I took a note from my mentor and business partner, cocktail queen Julie Reiner, and added some Martinique rhum as well, to bring up the floral funkiness even further.

Add all the ingredients, except the sugarcane stick, orchid, mint sprig, and lime wheel, to a cocktail shaker with ice. Shake briefly and strain over crushed or pebbled ice in a large rocks glass. Traditionally, this is garnished with a sugarcane stick and an edible orchid, so feel free to include them if you're feeling especially tropical. Otherwise, simply garnish with a mint sprig and lime wheel tucked inside the glass.

JUNGLE SLOW CRUISE

1 oz Appleton
Reserve Rum

¾ oz Pierre
Ferrand Cognac

¼ oz Wray & Nephew
Overpoof Rum

¼ Cruzan Black Strap Rum

½ oz Campari

¾ oz pineapple juice

½ oz lime juice

¼ oz Passion Fruit Syrup
(see page 150)

½ oz Cane Syrup
(see page 240)

Pineapple wedge and
2 fronds for garnish

This cocktail is an homage to a flat tire I got while trying to make it to the Appleton distillery in the center of the island of Jamaica. While Shannon Sturgis, the photographer for this book, and I were driving up and over mountains, following (idiotically) Google Maps, we ended up on the skinniest, most pockmarked "road" of all time. Driving white-knuckled around a blind corner (on the "wrong side" of the road, mind you!) I walloped a pothole and nearly sent us tumbling down the steep ravine of the tropical mountain. Of course, the spare tire with which Avis had supplied us was conveniently flat, so Shannon and I went on a two-hour drive with a very nice family through the Jamaican bush attempting to find a fix. Fortunately, we eventually did—buying the baldest tire I've ever seen from a man who made me write my own receipt on a page from a daily planner from 1967. This was the drink we were both craving toward the end. It's inspired by Leyenda bartender Ryan Liloia's riff on a tiki classic, the Jungle Bird: tall, tropical, slightly bitter, and refreshing.

Add all the ingredients, except the pineapple wedge and fronds, to a cocktail shaker with ice. Shake briefly and strain into a Collins glass with crushed or pebbled ice. Garnish with the pineapple wedge and fronds on the side of the glass.

QUITE RIGHTLY

Two 1-inch slices of yellow bell pepper

1 oz Rhum J.M Blanc

¾ oz Chairman's Reserve Rum

½ oz Wölffer Estate Verjus

½ oz Yellow Chartreuse

½ tsp Giffard Crème de Pêche

3 drops Bittermans Orchard Street Celery Shrub

1 dash Saline Tincture (see page 243)

Thinly sliced cucumber for garnish

St. Lucia has a unique colonial history. Being in line of sight both of French Martinique and the then-English Barbados, the island was fiercely fought over by the two powers when they were at war, and ultimately changed hands *fourteen* times between them before gaining its independence in 1979. The back-and-forth cultural influence of England and France is not only literally visible in St. Lucia today—the oldest buildings there are literally constructed in alternating French and English styles—but it's also tasted in its approach to rum, which emphasizes experimentation and variety.

One morning during a visit to St. Lucia, I woke up decently foggy after a night spent dancing and drinking horrific rum punches at their weekly Friday affair, the Jump Up. Groggily, I strolled down to the beach with SPIRIBAM's Ben Jones, my guide on the trip, to take a dip in the beautiful ocean to wash away the cobwebs. From our idyllic swimming hole, Martinique was just in sight. This drink, incorporating a blend of St. Lucia and Martinique r(h)ums, commemorates that amazing morning and that interesting theory.

Muddle the yellow bell pepper slices in the bottom of a mixing glass. Add all the other ingredients, except for the cucumber, with ice and stir. Strain into a Nick and Nora glass. Garnish with the slice of cucumber wrapped inside the glass.

MAIDEN NAME

2 oz Avuá Prata Cachaça

½ oz lime juice

½ oz coconut milk

¾ oz Vanilla Syrup
(see page 243)

¼ oz Cinnamon Bark
Syrup (see page 241)

¼ oz Passion Fruit Syrup
(recipe follows)

Freshly grated nutmeg
for garnish

2 pineapple fronds
for garnish

Edible orchid for garnish
(optional)

I adore piña coladas and could basically drink them all day, every day, any day. In making this variant, I wanted to amplify the basic recipe a little. Rather than using a light rum that doesn't bring much to the fat of the coconut, I used a more flavorful cachaça. I also elected to ditch the pineapple and obtain my fruit notes from passion fruit instead.

Add all the ingredients, except the nutmeg, pineapple fronds, and orchid, to a blender with a cup of ice and blend until smooth and integrated. Pour into a tiki mug or Collins glass. Garnish with freshly grated nutmeg, the pineapple fronds, and orchid (if using) placed inside the glass.

PASSION FRUIT SYRUP

3 oz Perfect Purée
passion fruit puree

1 oz superfine sugar

MAKES 4 OZ · Combine the ingredients in a blender, blend until dissolved and integrated, and bottle. Store in the refrigerator for up to 1 month.

TI PUNCH

2 lime discs (cut to have a little meat for juice but a lot of skin for bitterness)

1 tsp Rhum J.M Cane Syrup

2 oz Rhum J.M Blanc 55

This classic rhum cocktail was originally imbibed by fieldworkers in the French Caribbean to fortify them during the workday. Now, though, everyone in the French West Indies makes it in his or her own way, and everyone has opinions (and strong ones) about how it should be made. When I was in Martinique, I asked why there were so many different ways of making the classic drink. In response I was told the famous expression, *Chacun prepare sa propre mort* ("Everyone prepares his own death")—and that was enough for me! Whether you use granular sugar or syrup, ice or none, aged or blanc rhum, the mixture is your very own, and up to you. I prefer mine with a little sugar and a little ice.

Express the lime discs into a rocks glass with a few pieces of hand-cracked ice and then add the syrup and rhum. Stir slightly to chill and integrate and serve.

RUM POPO

2 oz Appleton Estate
21 Year Old Jamaica Rum

1 key lime, cut in half

The first drink I ever learned how to make was a Rum Popo, I made for my mother just as soon as she was comfortable letting me or my sister handle a knife. During that time, whenever we were on vacation, my mother would always get a few bottles of Appleton Rum (the good old stuff) for the house, and after a day of basic bliss on the beach (or wherever we were), she would ask one of us to run and make her a Popo.

Essentially modeled after a Ti Punch (see facing page); (not that Mama knew what that was), this simplest of drinks was named after her late dog—Malcolm X John Lennon, or Popo for short—who died before I was born.

It goes to show that if the base spirit is good it takes very little to make it a cocktail.

Add the rum to a rocks glass over ice, squeeze the lime halves in, and stir to dilute before serving.

FLIP YOUR TRADE

1 whole egg

1 oz El Dorado 15 Year Old Special Reserve Rum

½ oz Macallan Double Cask 12 Year Old Scotch Whisky

½ oz El Maestro Sierra Pedro Ximénez Sherry

½ oz J. Rieger & Co. Caffè Amaro

¼ oz Hampden Estate Pure Single Jamaican Rum

½ oz Cane Syrup (see page 240)

4 dashes House Aromatic Bitters (see page 241)

Freshly grated nutmeg for garnish

3 coffee beans

When I set out to create this cocktail, I wanted to conceptually link the trade routes of the first colonial trips from the "Old World" to the "New World" and back again. What I ended up with (somewhat surprisingly) was a variation on the historic Flip cocktail, a drink whose recipe dates back to Prohibition and includes— yes—a whole egg. This eggnog-reminiscent cocktail is an after-dinner drink, to be sure. A rich decadent affair.

Crack the egg into a cocktail shaker and discard the shell. Add all other ingredients, except the nutmeg and coffee beans, to the shaker and dry shake to emulsify the egg. Add ice, shake, and fine-strain into a coupe glass. Garnish with the nutmeg and coffee beans floated on top.

FEELINGS CATCHER

¾ oz Elijah Craig
Bourbon Whiskey

¾ oz Lustau Solera
Reserva Brandy

½ oz Coruba Jamaica Rum

½ oz lemon juice

½ oz Guava Syrup
(recipe follows)

¾ oz Donn's Mix
(recipe follows)

5 to 6 dashes
Peychaud's Bitters

Mint sprig for garnish

Jamaica is a truly beautiful island that holds so much more than the all-inclusive resorts of Negril and Montego Bay would suggest. In my youth, practically the only place I ever experienced besides Vermont's Green Mountains were the Blue Mountains on the northeast coast of Jamaica in the Portland Parish, far from cruise ships and their crisply sunburned patrons. My parents, who worked all year, would escape there with my twin sister and me for weeks at a time when we were little, adding up to years of my life spent there. Lena, the woman who helped raise us, gave me some of my first foods from this tropical island, including guava.

This tiki-inspired drink takes its inspiration from the tropical notes that aging spirits draw out of barrels. Bourbon plays nicely with the brandy and the light funk and richness of the Jamaican rum. It's the guava, though, that ties the rum together with the other ingredients.

Add all the ingredients, except the bitters and the mint sprig, to a cocktail shaker with ice. Shake briefly and strain over crushed or pebbled ice in a Pilsner glass or Collins glass. Float the bitters on top and garnish with the mint sprig.

GUAVA SYRUP

4 oz Perfect Purée
pink guava puree

4 oz superfine sugar

MAKES 7 OZ · Combine the ingredients in a blender. Blend until dissolved and integrated. Transfer to an airtight container. Store in the refrigerator for up to 1 month.

DONN'S MIX

2 oz grapefruit juice

1 oz Cinnamon Bark
Syrup (see page 241)

MAKES 3 OZ · Combine the ingredients in a glass and stir to fully incorporate. Store in the refrigerator for up to 4 days.

STIR KEY

1 oz Smith & Cross
Jamaica Rum

½ oz Gosling's Rum

½ oz Cruzan
BlackStrap Rum

¼ oz Orgeat Works
Macadamia Nut
Orgeat Syrup

2 dashes House Aromatic
Bitters (see page 241)

Orange twist for garnish

Camper English, a cocktail writer hailing from San Francisco, came into the bar I was working at one day about a decade ago and requested something "stirred and murky." My head went right to rum, along with a few of the other densest flavors I could think of. Rum is very traditionally blended. Some buy rum the world over from different distilleries, do a little rum mixology, and bottle the resulting liquid as new, no heavy lifting of fermenting or distilling at all. I like to achieve that in cocktails by blending my own. With this resulting Stir Key cocktail, the funkiness of the Jamaican Smith & Cross gets muddied (in a good way!) by the rich blackstrap and Gosling's rum. The orange twist brightens it up just enough.

Add all the ingredients, except the orange twist, to a mixing glass with ice and stir. Strain over a large ice cube in a rocks glass. Express the oils of the orange twist over the glass and place the twist inside the glass.

SHADOW BOXER

1½ oz Yaguara Cachaça

¾ oz Campari

¾ oz Dolin Dry Vermouth

¼ oz Blume Marillen Apricot Eau-de-Vie

¼ oz Giffard Pamplemousse Liqueur

Orange twist for garnish

This cocktail started as yet another Negroni variation, but ended up something very much its own thing and a staple for us at Leyenda. The cachaça I selected here is a blend of an unaged silver with a touch of European oak, which lends itself well to the bitter sweetness of the Campari. The dry vermouth carries the apricot eau de vie to bring out the cachaça's rich fruit even further, and the pamplemousse liqueur comes in to link everything back to the citrus of the Campari.

Add all the ingredients, except the orange twist, to a mixing glass and stir. Strain over a large ice cube in a rocks glass. Express the oils of the orange twist over the glass and place the twist inside the glass.

KINGDOM COME

1½ oz Damoiseau Rhum Agricole 110 proof

½ oz Cappelletti Aperitivo

¾ oz lime juice

1¼ oz Watermelon Syrup (see page 89)

Spicy Salt (recipe follows)

1 lime twist

This one's a watermelon daiquiri with a kick. I decided to use a rhum agricole from the French West Indies isle of Guadaloupe to bring some proof and slightly vegetal and mineral notes to the watermelon syrup I used. The wine-based Italian bitter serves as a period at the end of the drink.

Damoiseau is a classic bottle seen on back bars of local watering holes lining the beautiful beaches of Guadeloupe. As in much of the West Indies, like Wray and Nephew in Jamaica, high proof runs the show. When we finally got it in the States, I was thrilled to use the Guadeloupen classic in this crushable sipper.

Add all the ingredients, except the spicy salt and the lime twist, to a cocktail shaker with ice. Wet the rim of a coupe glass with the lime twist and roll the glass in the spicy salt. Shake the cocktail and fine-strain into the glass. Express the oils of the lime twist over the glass and then discard the twist.

SPICY SALT

2 Tbsp superfine sugar

1 Tbsp ground pink peppercorns

1 Tbsp salt

YIELDS 4 TBSP · Add the sugar, pink peppercorns, and salt to a bowl and stir to integrate. Store in an airtight jar in a cool dry place indefinitely.

DESDE SIEMPRE

1½ oz Uruapan Charanda
Mexican Aguardiente

¾ oz Rhine Hall
Mango Brandy

½ oz Hans Reisetbauer
Carrot Eau di Vie

½ tsp Cane Syrup
(see page 240)

2 dashes Saline Tincture
(see page 243)

Lime twist for garnish

Charanda is a sugarcane aguardiente, hailing from the lush microclimate in Michoacan, Mexico. As it turns out, the land of some of Mexico's greatest mezcales has some great terrain for sugarcane, too! The name of Uruapan, the city from which charanda hails, essentially means "the land of eternal spring" or "where the trees are always flowering" in the area's native language, and that's exactly what it is. This quaint city is a far cry from the vast sandy deserts of the north, and it is nestled next to the Cupatitzio River, whose abundant swimming holes are perfect places to sip this awesome spirit, if you get a chance.

Charanda is made from fresh sugarcane juice, so it has some of that residual oily funk and full fall-fruit notes that you find in some cachaças and rhum agricoles. Here, I wanted to let the rum stand up for itself, so I used the mango brandy to highlight its fruit notes and the carrot to emphasize its slight funk and earthiness.

Add all the ingredients, except the lime twist, to a mixing glass with ice and stir. Strain over a large ice cube in a rocks glass. Express the oils of the lime twist over the glass and then place the twist on the rim of the glass.

PANCHO PERICO

Banana leaf for garnish

1¼ oz Duquesne Blanc Agricole Rhum

¾ oz Elijah Craig Bourbon Whiskey

½ oz La Guita Manzanilla Sherry

1¼ oz Poblano Syrup (recipe follows)

½ oz pineapple juice

¾ oz lime juice

Lime wheel for garnish

This drink, by Shannon Ponche of Leyenda, is a tall, slightly spicy stunner. We traditionally garnish it with a banana leaf for visual effect, but it's not necessary. The bright-green color speaks for itself.

This cocktail proved itself a gateway to rhum agricole. If you're perhaps skeptical of its deliciousness, whip this up to change your mind.

Spiral the banana leaf into a Collins glass and add crushed or pebbled ice. Add all the other ingredients, except the lime wheel, to a cocktail shaker with ice. Shake briefly and strain over the ice in the Collins glass. After pouring the drink, top it with fresh ice and garnish with the lime wheel.

POBLANO SYRUP

8 poblano peppers, stemmed but not seeded

1 cup agave nectar

MAKES 3 CUPS • Using a juice extractor, juice the poblanos to yield about 2 cups of juice. Add the juice and agave nectar to a blender, blend until integrated, and bottle. Store in the refrigerator for up to 2 weeks.

BACK AT YA

½ lime, sliced into quarters

¼ oz Cane Syrup
(see page 240)

½ oz Avua
Balsamo Cachaça

1 oz Aperol

½ oz Yaguara Cachaça

½ oz pineapple juice

4 to 5 spritzes
Sandalwood Tincture
(recipe follows)

This drink was inspired by a trip to Brazil where I got to do a deep dive into the various local woods used for aging cachaça. I went to the incredibly quaint but (to me) rather bizarre town of Ivoti in Rio Grande do Sul. This town, populated almost entirely by German descendants, looks more like Bavaria than what you might think of as Brazil. Brazil is a massive and wonderfully diverse country; and this town with its German-speaking, blond Brazilians is just an example!

In Ivoti, unsurprisingly, they bring a German precision to their cachaça. While there, I visited the distillery of Weber Haus, home of Yaguarsa Cachaça and, after trying some amazing cachaça aged in balsam wood, I decided I would try to make an amplified Caipirinha with it back at home.

Muddle the lime quarters in the cane syrup in a cocktail shaker. Add the cachaça and Aperol, shake hard, and pour with the pineapple juice into a rocks glass (no ice). Spritz the sandalwood tincture on top.

SANDALWOOD TINCTURE

6 drops sandalwood oil

8 oz Polmos Spirytus
Rektyfikowany

MAKES 8 OZ · In a blender, combine the sandalwood oil and Spirytus and blend for 30 seconds on high speed. Store in an airtight jar in a cool dry place indefinitely.

CHILLER INSTINCT

2 oz Michter's US*1 Kentucky Straight Bourbon Whiskey

½ oz Lustau East India Solera Sherry

1 tsp Giffard Crème de Fruits de la Passion

1 tsp Cinnamon Bark Syrup (see page 241)

1 tsp Licor 43

Lemon twist for garnish

Ryan Liloia created this variation on the traditional Old Fashioned for Leyenda. Passion fruit is usually left for bright, tropical drinks that we'd sip by the pool. But in this stirred drink, he paired it wonderfully with the Licor 43's vanilla notes and the cinnamon and sherry. This is a real celebration of bourbon, but in an unconventional tiki/Leyenda-esque way.

Add all the ingredients, except the lemon twist, to a mixing glass with ice and stir. Strain over a large ice cube in a rocks glass. Express the oils of the lemon twist over the glass and then place the twist inside the glass.

BROOKLYN BURRO

2 oz Plantation 3 Stars
White Rum

½ oz lime juice

½ oz pineapple juice

½ oz Ginger Syrup
(recipe follows)

2 dashes Angostura
Aromatic Bitters

1 oz soda water

Lime wheel for garnish

Candied ginger
for garnish

This Moscow Mule variation is an attempt to give the
vodka-based classic a little Latin flavor. With the addition
of pineapple and bitters, this light drink is a familiar favorite
made foreign yet again. A menu staple at Leyenda, it's a
crowd-pleaser but you can easily substitute other spirits to
play around.

**Add all the ingredients, except the soda water, the lime
wheel, and the candied ginger, to a cocktail shaker with
ice. Shake and strain over fresh ice in a rocks glass. Top
with the soda water and garnish with a cocktail pick
through the lime wheel and candied ginger.**

GINGER SYRUP

About five 1-inch cubes
fresh ginger

1 cup superfine sugar

MAKES 6 OZ • In a juice extractor, juice the ginger to yield
4 ounces (do not worry about peeling the ginger). Combine the
juice and sugar in a saucepan over low heat; stir until the sugar
is dissolved. Remove from the heat immediately, allow to cool,
and then bottle. Store in the refrigerator for up to 4 weeks.

TRUTH FICTION

¾ oz Rittenhouse
Rye Whiskey

¾ oz Plantation
Pineapple Rum

½ oz Novo Fogo
Barrel-Aged Cachaça

½ oz Contratto
Bitter Liqueur

½ tsp Demerara Syrup
(see page 241)

5 to 6 spritzes
Sandalwood Tincture
(see page 166)

1 lemon twist

I first became interested in working with wood flavors after a visit to my favorite spot in Shoreditch, London, Sager + Wilde. They had two wood-flavored drinks on the menu, one of which (flavored with cedar) I completely fell in love with. The aromatics reminded me of the time in my late teens and early twenties living throughout Guatemala and other parts of Latin America, I developed a very strong interest in Catholicism and spent many hours in churches there.

I'd come to appreciate the smell of cathedrals in particular—of musty incense, carved wood, and old books—and I wanted to create a drink inspired by that smell. Taking sandalwood as my starting point, I went down through its distinct tasting notes and put together a group of other ingredients that supported those flavors.

Combine all the ingredients, except the sandalwood tincture and lemon twist, in a mixing glass with ice and then stir. Spritz the inside of a chilled rocks glass with the tincture. Strain the cocktail into the spritzed glass (with no ice, sazerac style). Express the oils of the lemon twist over the glass and then discard the twist.

EL VIEJUCO

1 oz Rittenhouse
Rye Whiskey

¾ oz El Dorado
12-Year Old Rum

¼ oz Smith & Cross Rum

¼ oz Tempus Fugit
Crème de Cacao

1 dash Dale DeGroff's
Pimento Aromatic Bitters

1 dash House Orange
Bitters (see page 242)

4 to 5 spritzes
Fernet Branca

Orange twist for garnish

Bartender Amanda de la Nuez created this drink at Leyenda, combining her love of whiskey with her love of rum. The bright rye gives a little backbone to the English-style rum, and the heavy pot-stilled Jamaican rum lends it back some wonderful body. This Old Fashioned–like drink is rich and complex.

Add all the ingredients, except the Fernet Branca and the orange twist, to a mixing glass with ice and stir. Strain over a large ice cube in a rocks glass and add the Fernet Branca on top. Express the oils of the orange twist over the glass and place the twist inside the glass.

LAGRIMAS ROJAS

SERVES 4 OR 5

10 oz Malbec red wine

3¾ oz Appleton Estate
Signature Blend Rum

2½ oz Smith & Cross Rum

1 oz Tempus Fugit
Crème de Cacao

¾ oz St. Elizabeth
Allspice Dram

2½ oz maple syrup

2½ oz lemon juice

3¾ oz orange juice

4 lemon wheels
for garnish

4 orange quarters
for garnish

This drink was actually inspired by my trips to Spain, in particular to the south, where one can sit in a terraza for hours, alternately sipping sangria and espressos. This autumnal sangria-like pitcher is meant to be made in a big batch, from which guests are invited to serve themselves. To make it more Leyenda-esque, I chose to use an Argentinian Malbec and gave it some fortification and character with two different Jamaican rums. It's slightly funky, with a little chocolate hint playing against the allspice.

Have an appropriate number of small glasses with ice ready for pouring. Add all the ingredients, except the lemon wheels and orange quarters, to a pitcher with ice. Stir to dilute. Garnish the glasses (and pitcher) with the lemon wheels and orange quarters.

PAN AM SOUR

1¼ oz Elijah Craig
Bourbon Whiskey

¾ oz Avuá Prata Cachaça

¾ oz Simple Syrup
(see page 243)

¼ oz orange juice

½ oz Malbec red wine

Shortly after Leyenda opened, our friend David Wondrich, noted cocktail historian, came in with his wife, Karen, for a drink and a hello. I was behind the bar and upon hearing that Dave wanted, "You know, whatever," I decided to go to one of his all-time favorites, the New York Sour from when I worked across the street at the Clover Club. I reworked it Leyenda-style. Dave named the resulting drink himself, after the defunct airline on which he'd once traveled the Americas.

Add all the ingredients, except the wine, to a cocktail shaker with ice. Shake and fine-strain into a coupe glass. Gently pour the Malbec over a spoon to float a layer of wine on top of the drink.

MOONTOWER

2 oz Plantation
Pineapple Rum

1½ oz Wölffer Estate Verjus

¼ oz Smith & Cross Rum

¼ oz Pineapple Syrup
(see page 242)

1 lime twist

Rarely, I think, does a drink come along that's at once so simple and so celebratory of the spirit around which it's made. Jesse Harris created this drink out of love for Plantation Pineapple Rum, and it shows. This rum has a cult following within the cocktail community and seems to make something delicious out of anything and everything it is added to— but what about when it's the star of the show? With just a little highly funky Jamaican rum to up the rummy-ness and some acid from the verjus, this cocktail drinks as though a pineapple daiquiri and a Manhattan had a baby together.

Add all the ingredients, except the lime twist, to a mixing glass with ice and then stir. Strain into a Nick and Nora glass. Express the oils of the lime twist over the glass and then discard the twist.

CLEARLY FAR AFFAIR

1 oz Clairin Sajous

½ oz La Guita
Manzanilla Sherry

½ oz Lemorton Pommeau

1 oz Granny Smith
apple juice

½ oz Demerara Syrup
(see page 241)

½ oz lemon juice

2 dashes Cardamom
Tincture (see page 240)

1 dash Saline Tincture
(see page 243)

1 oz Isastegi Sagardo
Naturala Basque Cider

3 thin apple slices
for garnish

I think clairin is one of the most interesting spirits out there, and my trip spent driving the expanse of Haiti and visiting the diversity of people and cultures there was so vibrant and unusual, I still fall back on it as the source of many cocktail inspirations. The country really does make a spirit as expressive and unique as its people.

The Sajous clairin I use here tastes simultaneously of grass and green mango, and I pair it with the acidity of the apple juice, using some pommeau for more richness and cardamom and saline to bring back the tartness of the apple skins.

Add all the ingredients, except the cider and the apple slices, to a cocktail shaker with ice. Shake and strain into a Collins glass. Top with the cider and garnish with the apple slices rotated out to create a fan.

CUBA LIBRE

2 lime wedges

2 oz Havana Club
3 Year Old Rum

½ oz Kola Syrup
(facing page)

3 oz soda water

When I opened Leyenda, I became obsessed with Coca-Cola and the history behind it after hearing an NPR special. Latin America (led by Mexico) consumes more of the stuff than any other region on the planet, and it's mixed with just about every alcohol consumed there to make a quick cocktail.

The most popular of these mixtures is the Cuba Libre. This drink came to be in Cuba after the Spanish-American war, when Coca-Cola came in swinging to make money there. For this drink, I teamed up with tiki genius and rum mastermind Jelani Johnson to create our own Kola Syrup—a process that took far more research and development than any other drink on our menu, totaling more than 21 hours. We subbed out the original recipe's classic cocaine for a slightly more legal mate reduction to complement the kola nut. You can use it in the Cuba Libre, in a Chilean Piscola, in Argentina's famous Fernet and Coke, a Batanga with tequila, and so on. It's labor intensive, but worth it! I was thrilled Jelani agreed to share this work.

Squeeze a lime wedge in the bottom of a highball glass and top with ice. Add all the other ingredients, except the lime wedge, and stir to integrate. Garnish with the reserved lime wedge on the rim of the glass.

KOLA SYRUP

3 cups white sugar

2 tsp dark brown sugar

2 cups water

1 vanilla bean, sliced open

2 star anise (crunched up)

1 tsp juniper berries

1 tsp coarsely smashed (not pulverized) cinnamon bark

3 tsp minced ginger

2 whole smashed (not pulverized) nutmeg

Zest of 1 lemon

Zest of 1 lime

Zest of 1 orange

8 oz lime juice

6 tsp kola extract*

4 tsp mate extract**

1 oz Angostura Aromatic Bitters

2 tsp phosphoric acid

1½ tsp molasses

MAKES 1 QT · Add both sugars, the water, vanilla bean, star anise, juniper berries, cinnamon bark, ginger, nutmeg, and all the zests to a pot and bring to a simmer over medium heat; cook for 10 minutes. Allow to cool overnight (about 10 hours). Run through a chinois strainer and add the lime juice, kola extract, mate extract, Angostura bitters, phosphoric acid, and molasses and stir. Transfer to an airtight container. Store in the refrigerator for up to 1 month.

*Kola extract—Grind kola nuts to obtain 4 Tbsp of the powder. Add this to 7 oz Polmos Spirytus Rektyfikowany and allow to sit for 20 minutes. Strain through a coffee filter into an airtight container. Lasts indefinitely.

**Mate extract—Add 1 cup of mate loose-leaf tea to 7 oz Polmos Spirytus Rektyfikowany and allow to sit for 20 minutes. Strain through a coffee filter into an airtight container. Lasts indefinitely.

LIME IN TI COCONUT

2 oz Coconut-Infused
Clément Rhum Canne
Bleue (recipe follows)

½ oz Cesar Florido
Fino Sherry

½ oz Dolin Blanc
Vermouth de Chambery

½ tsp Vanilla Syrup
(see page 243)

2 dashes Saline Tincture
(see page 243)

Lime twist for garnish

Leanne Favre took the dare of creating her own Ti Punch variation for a summer Leyenda menu, and really knocked it out of the park by marrying that classic with another one: the martini. The rhum in this drink is made specifically out of blue sugarcane, a particularly delicious treat that is only helped by the additional process of a coconut fat-washing.

Add all the ingredients, except the lime twist, to a mixing glass with ice and then stir. Strain over a large ice cube in a rocks glass. Express the oils of the lime twist over the glass and place the twist in the glass.

COCONUT-INFUSED CLÉMENT RHUM CANNE BLEUE

2 Tbsp coconut oil

750 ml Clément Rhum
Canne Bleue

MAKES 750 ML · Add the coconut oil and rhum to a food-safe container. Whisk together to integrate and let sit in open air for 4 hours. Cover and place in the freezer overnight (about 10 hours). The next day, strain off the frozen solidified oil through a cheesecloth. Store in the refrigerator indefinitely.

GRAPE

Above: Showing off prized grapes at a harvest festival in Tarija, Bolivia. **Page 182:** Fieldworker Margarita Constancio harvests grapes for singani in Tarija, Bolivia.

In 2018, I gave a seminar on Latin American spirits at a cocktail festival in London. Among other topics, I spoke about Latin American grape spirits such as pisco and singani, which I find hugely undervalued. During the Q&A after my talk, a strange thing happened: every one of the questions that came up—100 percent of the Q&A—had to do with the argument over pisco's national origin. It was clear that the question of whether pisco was *really* Peruvian or *really* Chilean was something that a lot of my audience was concerned about, and perhaps, I sensed, even willing to fight over. I pointed this out and was surprised to learn that about a third of my audience was either Peruvian or Chilean, and had a serious personal investment in the issue at hand.

I was dumbfounded. Despite the fact that most people outside of South America have probably never tasted this stuff, Chileans and Peruvians can get into a heated argument over it—at a friendly conference overseas! Clearly, I had some learning to do . . . as do we all.

Grape-based aguardientes—particularly the aforementioned pisco and singani—are, in my humble opinion, the most accessible Latin American spirit. Why? Well, for starters, they're clear (hello, vodka fans!) and pretty floral (St. Germain, anyone?), so when well made, they're the epitome of an easy-drinking spirit. They're the closest that Latin spirits get to what most of us know well already, which is why drinkers outside of Latin America, when trying them for the first time, often wonder, "Why haven't I been drinking this all along?"

And for the most part, most of us haven't been. Grape distillates from Latin America represent a major hole in today's global spirits consciousness. Even pisco, once extremely popular in America—central, in fact, to the classic cocktail era on which the recent cocktail revival is based—has remained a relative secret in the United States since Prohibition. This fact becomes even stranger when we consider the soaring popularity of grape spirits in South America: not only are they consumed very widely there, but (as proven by my seminar audience) they are very often liquid representations of South American national identity.

So how is it that this family of spirits can mean so much to the people who make it, can once have meant so much to Americans, and can be so wonderfully accessible to our palates and yet remain essentially unknown outside of South America today?

In my opinion, the key to answering all of these questions lies in the fact that these spirits—more so than any of the others we have discussed in this book—are a European import. Unlike agave spirits (created from endemic plants, via European-inspired techniques) or sugarcane spirits (chaotic cultural mashups of European, American, and African influences), grape-based aguardientes, and the grapes they're made from, were brought over to Latin America by European colonists, and produced in the Americas in imitation of already-existing distillates back home. This is what makes them so accessible, and once made them so popular, to non-Latin drinkers. It's what makes them beloved in the countries where they're made—countries that still today hold their European colonial influence in esteem—even to the point of being a matter of national identity. And ultimately, it's what has allowed them to fall off the radar elsewhere, over an interesting and turbulent history.

HISTORY

From the beginning, grapes and grape-based beverages were a matter of religious importance to the European colonists. The earliest of these colonists were, of course, Catholics; and in their many journeys across the Atlantic and farther down the Americas, they made it a priority to set up missions practically everywhere they stopped. In the operation of these missions, an essential ingredient was the Blood of Christ itself: wine. But the grapes from which that wine was made were not available in the Americas, so right along with the establishment of each mission came the cultivation and growing of grapevines—or at least the attempt to do so.

It was Hernán Cortés who led the Spanish conquistadores first to Mexico and then south in the early 1500s; and it was he who first brought grapes with him to ensure that there would be enough wine for the Holy Communion to transform the areas' indigenous populations into good, God-fearing—and presumably Cortés-fearing—Christians. (Even so, the new religion was often rejected by indigenous populations. In order to convince their people to pray to the image of the Virgin Mary, for example, Incan priests resorted to secretly inserting sacred llama bones into the effigies to make them divine in their own terms.) After a few less-than-stellar (and far too hot) farming attempts from Hispaniola to Mexico and farther south, the conquistadores finally found the right soil and climate for the vines on the western coast of South America. (Those other enthusiastic Catholic colonists, the Portuguese, also brought grapes with them to Brazil, by way of Madeira and the Azores, only a few years after the Spanish arrived; but it was in the valleys of what would become present-day Peru that wine production first really took off.)

Of course, Señor Cortés wasn't by any means setting eyes on virgin South American soil. The land had already been well developed, long before Europeans arrived. The Norte Chico civilization, which occupied modern-day Peru from almost 4000 BC, is one of the oldest civilizations in the world; other well-established tribes and communities were already flourishing across South America, including the Cañari in Ecuador; the Inca, Moche, or Chavín of the Andes; and the Arawak of the continent's eastern coast. These millions of pre-Columbian peoples were skilled farmers, and, as anyone who has visited Machu Picchu can attest, they possessed an exceptional knowledge of how to work the land. (And how to make alcohol, it turns out. The Incans who inhabited the land long before Columbus and his descendants arrived, for example, were partial to the *chicha* they made from fermented corn; the clay vessels they used to store it would later be adopted by wine and grape-spirits producers.)

In the early days of colonization, these grapes were mostly used to create the most basic form of mission wine; not so much the $500 bottle you might covet in your basement for a special occasion, so much as the kind of stuff kids buy in college by the jug. Bad wine then was as bad as it remains today, and mission wine, which didn't have to satisfy a lot of requirements besides being the blood of Christ, was basically that. But after centuries of voyages and viti-cultural operations—and an increasing population with more than sacramental drinking on the agenda moved in—many more grape varietals were brought to the continent, and much, much better wines were made there.

Catholicism radiated out through South America with colonial expansion to Argentina, Chile, and beyond, and the holy grape came with it. The sixteenth century saw the birth of more than six hundred parochial towns across the continent, particularly in the area encompassing modern-day Bolivia, Peru, and Chile. In the second half of that century, the valleys of

Fog rolls into a valley of neat rows of grapevines. Bodega Casa Real, Tarija, Bolivia.

Arequipa (in what is now Peru) became the center of the most prolific wine production in the whole region, and the area became the largest wine producer in Latin America, causing the colonists to ship the wine back home because of the abundance. But they produced so much of the stuff that, in 1641, King Philip IV of Spain imposed a heavy tax on "New World" wine exports in an effort to stop them from competing with wine producers back in Europe. This effectively banned the exportation of colonial wine and left winemakers with a lot of unsellable product on their hands—which caused said winemakers to focus more of their attention on distillation to go through the surplus of rapidly spoiling wine.

The concept for the earliest Latin grape spirit—the production of which is said to have preceded that of cognac—had been brought over by the Galician Spanish missionaries as an elaboration on their own Spanish grape distillate, *orujo*. The Spanish brought over the same copper-pot alembic stills they had been using at home. With them, they produced the first grape spirits in Latin America, drank them mightily in the colonies, and shipped them back out to Europe via ports along the western coast of the continent. The new grape spirit adopted the name *pisco*, and the reason for this name, along with exactly when and where its production first occurred, is still the center of a nationalistic debate.

The seventeenth century saw much of South America coming into its own as an attractive, largely self-sustaining industrial center, and the production of wine and spirits ramped up to help quench the thirst of the rapidly expanding expatriate population. The great Cerro Rico ("rich mountain") of Potosí, in the area of central South America that is now Bolivia, was "discovered" in 1545 by Spanish conquistadores, and produced silver in such abundance that there was said to be enough to build a bridge from Potosí to Spain. Once word of the silver spread, prospectors arrived in droves from around the world to resettle in Bolivia and beyond. The impact of Potosí on the regional economy was overwhelming, and by the mid-seventeenth century, Potosí had a larger population than any city in the Americas—or most of the capitals in Europe, for that matter. As is true of most economically booming times, the Bolivian silver rush was opulent, celebratory, and thirsty—and it was grapes that satisfied many the parched palate. With the arrival on the continent of more and more people from Europe came an increasing desire for better wines and spirits, and more and more grapes from Europe made their way over to the welcoming soil of South America.

Being popular at home is great, but it's really demand abroad that boosts both pride in a product and the market for it that puts it on the map. For South American grape spirits, the gold rush in the western territories of the United States did just that. When gold was discovered in California in the mid-nineteenth century, many of the experienced laborers from the mining-heavy regions of modern-day Bolivia and Peru migrated north and brought with them their thirst for grape distillates. Pisco became the drink of choice for many Pacific Coast miners—South American, North American, or otherwise—and producers began to ship it up in bulk to meet their demand.

The advent of the Pisco Punch, created at The Bank Exchange Saloon in San Francisco in the mid-1850s, solidified the spirit's place in cocktail history. From its inception, the Pisco Punch was a status drink, concocted from secret ingredients and sold at a high price to celebrity imbibers such as Mark Twain. With the popularity of the cocktail soaring, pisco became more sought-after than ever Stateside, and demand for it continued to grow through the end of the nineteenth century.

But the good times couldn't last forever. With the subsequent crash of the U.S. economy and the blow dealt to its burgeoning cocktail culture by the passing of Prohibition, the American demand for pisco fell. Unlike other spirits from around the world however, pisco's popularity in America didn't return when Prohibition was lifted—and remarkably, it still hasn't, with the exception of a few enthusiasts, despite the universal cocktail revival of recent years. In large part, this was because Prohibition had focused American attention on two other, closer-in-proximity Latin spirits we've already mentioned, whose popularity continued to soar post-Prohibition: tequila and rum. Furthermore, after the mining years, South American trade routes were less frequently used than those to and from Europe; and the area's grape distillates were arguably too similar to European brandies to be worth taking the extra trouble for.

But the biggest reason that pisco and other grape distillates have taken this long to regain worldwide popularity has more to do with the modern history of the countries in which they are made, and the long period of unrest that not only curtailed the production and exportation of high-quality distillates but also brought about a destructive lack of unity among their producers that continues to this day.

It is in this turbulent modern history of South America that we find the beginnings of the still-burning question of *who* exactly has the right to claim pisco as their own. Peru and Chile each claim to have originated the spirit, and the argument touches some very deep nerves. (Bolivia kept itself out of that particular argument by sticking to its own signature grape spirit, singani; but in terms of the unrest of the area and its effects, Bolivia is very much part of the equation.) Understanding this history a bit better will enable us to see why, far more than a passing quibble, this question remains a matter of patriotism and national identity.

Chapacos celebrate the sale of their abundant harvest. Tarija, Bolivia.

Digging a bit deeper into the complex history of the region can make for a difficult task, particularly because the names and borders of the various countries and territories of South America have changed many times—and very significantly—in the five hundred years since their colonization, and even more so following their independence from the European colonial powers. But in explaining the complexity of who "owns" these spirits, the important thing to understand first is that once upon a time, Chile, Peru, and Bolivia were all considered part of one region under Spain's rule: a vast territory called the Viceroyalty of Peru. The way this viceroyalty eventually divided into smaller countries, particularly *these* three countries, forms the heart of the debate over territorial boundaries and national character that in many areas still rages today, involving everything from economics and racial politics to—yes—local foods and beverages.

The Viceroyalty of Peru, the most powerful of the four Spanish viceroyalties, was an institution created by the Spanish monarchy during the fifteenth century to facilitate government in its overseas territories. Viceroys were given the job to rule these vast new territories of the Spanish Empire, not as colonies, but as semi-independent imperial provinces, under the same laws and customs as applied in any other province back in Spain. With this viceroyalty, the Spanish expanded their empire enormously, most significantly due to the ample agricultural and mining resources for which the region quickly became famous.

It was during this time that the grape spirit we call pisco was first distilled. The name *pisco,* derived from an indigenous Quechua word for "bird," was also the name of a famous port town near the Ica Valley in present-day Peru, and many people (particularly the Peruvians) believe the spirit derives its name from that particularly grape-rich region. The Ica Valley, it is true, was famous by the eighteenth century for creating the best grape aguardientes in South America; and it is entirely logical that *pisco* began as a specific term for grape distillates from that area and later became the generic term for all grape distillates. In support of that theory, the Customs Guides of 1764 contain the first entries in which port workers, tired of laboriously entering the distillate as "aguardiente from the Pisco region," dropped the words "region" and "aguardiente" and simply wrote "pisco"—much as "brandy from Cognac, France" eventually just became "cognac."

So . . . simple, right? Pisco is Peruvian.

Well—not so fast, say many (mostly) Chileans.

For starters, because *pisco* was (until recently) a relatively generic word, other places back then had it in their names, too, including (gasp!) coastal areas in Chile—and the grape aguardiente *might* have come from one of them as well—or instead. Other ports, including ports in modern-day Chile, were also early distillers and exporters of grape spirits. Some scholars even believe that an ancient Chilean tribe, the Aymaras, were the first to make pisco in the Valle del Elqui—land that is now Chilean. (As with agave distillates in Mexico, there are even arguments that the Aymaras were distilling prior to the arrival of the Spanish.) Others cite an early written record of pisco in that area, dated 1733. The document is an inventory of goods registered after the death of one of the estate's owners; among them a massive vineyard, pot stills, and (most important) three *botijas de pisco*. According to pro-Chilean theorists, this registration of the clay cylindrical containers used to store the alcohol (themselves referred to as *piscos*) is why, from here on out, pisco was called *pisco*—in other words, the booze was named for the vessel, not for the port. (To which the Peruvians retort that the vessels themselves were made in Peru. But that doesn't stop the argument being made.) Furthermore, the Chileans were also the first to officially slap a label on a registered and commercially trademarked bottle of pisco, calling it by that name as early as 1882. (Peruvians took their time with that, only getting around to registering, labeling, and bottling pisco in 1922.)

In the end, the only thing everyone seems able to agree on is that the spirit originated, not in Peru or Chile as we know them today, but somewhere in the region that once encompassed both of them: the Viceroyalty of Peru. Also produced within that area—in the high mountains of present-day Bolivia—was the somewhat similar grape distillate singani, which Bolivia has long claimed as its national spirit. Originally produced, as legend has it, to give the people fortitude during the extremely cold Bolivian winters, singani is generally thought to have been named after a precolonial pueblo whose mission first distilled the spirit and traded it to the neighboring parched mining city of Potosí.

The territory of the Viceroyalty of Peru endured Spanish rule for only a few hundred years before it earned its independence through a series of revolutions in the first quarter of the nineteenth century. At this point, the Spanish fled north to attempt to regain strength in their only remaining American territories in the Caribbean, principally Puerto Rico and Cuba, while the people

Piscos, ancient clay containers used for storing the spirit of the same name. Subtanjalla, Ica, Peru.

in the newly independent countries of the south—by now largely a racial and cultural mestizo population—triumphantly declared their freedom from the Spanish. But no sooner had they achieved that independence than the territory underwent even more social and political upheaval, this time among the newly established South American nations.

In demarcating the new territories, the liberating general, Simón Bolívar, applied the principle of *uti possidetis juris* (literally, "as you possess under law"), and the borders of the three countries remained exactly what they'd been when the countries were colonial jurisdictions under the viceroyalty. This didn't work for long. After only a few decades, each of the new nations started to push for a redrawing of the boundaries, and the War of the Pacific broke out.

The War of the Pacific—an enormous South American national head-butting, in which Latin grape distillates and their origins came to be of patriotic significance—raged for five years, from 1879 to 1884. During that time, Chile fought against a Peru–Bolivia allied army, each power seeking territorial domi-nance of the mineral-rich areas in and around the Atacama Desert and, more important, of the trade-capable Pacific coast. Essentially, Chile didn't want Bolivia to be able to access the ocean ports without paying a tax; and when Peru came to defend its long-standing ally Bolivia—with which the country had enjoyed a good relationship since the days of the viceroyalty—Chile decimated both countries, gaining possession of the coastal territory and the lucrative mines with one fell swoop. The history of the twentieth century in these three countries is in many ways a testament to that victory: Chile's economy boomed and the country became an economic powerhouse, while Peru and Bolivia struggled, thus deepening their resentment of the Chilean victors.

Out of the War of the Pacific came a bitter strain of anti-Chilean senti-ment in Peru and Bolivia—a sentiment that lingers in those countries today. (Many people in both Peru and Bolivia still chalk up their countries' economic underdevelopment to Chile's seizure of their seaports and mines.) To make the situation even more volatile, the twentieth century brought infamous political turmoil to Central and South America, in the form of Marxist revolutionary struggles and the powerful drug cartels that arose to take advantage of the resulting instability. The economic and social turbulence that this caused in all three countries and beyond during that time was extreme and often strikingly similar from one nation to another.

LAND DISPUTES IN PERU

When I was visiting Peru in early 2019, I went out to some grape fields owned by artisanal producers. When we arrived, I got out of the car and strolled off on my own to look at the rows of grapes. Suddenly a group of farmers ran toward me, shouting madly and interrogating me about who I was and what I was doing there. They calmed down when they realized I was with Diego Loret de Mola, owner of BarSol Pisco, who was a longtime friend of theirs and buyer of their grapes.

As it turns out, what I'd experienced is shockingly commonplace in Peru today. Violent land disputes have arisen all over the country, an indirect result of the agrarian reforms the government implemented after the Marxist revolution of 1968. In nationalizing its farmlands, Peru's government appropriated the country's privately owned land and parceled it out to new farmers and families to work on, in an effort to ensure a more egalitarian distribution of labor and agricultural experience. In exchange, the original owners were given government bonds signifying that the land would return to them after fifty years.

Fast-forward fifty years to the present day, when families with claims on government land (generally wealthy and politically well-connected) are now coming forward to collect on their old titles. The problem is, reinstating land, even for the well-connected, requires a lengthy legal process—and the other people who have been working and living on that land for the last half-century are not in any mood to leave.

To get these farmers out more quickly, some of the more powerful groups have resorted to intimidation and theft, sending thugs around to attack the farmers. Grapes are often stolen from the vines at night, twenty or thirty kilos at a time. In response, farmers in many areas have been putting up fences, patrolling with guard dogs and banding together in armed militias. Tensions around the fields can run very high. It's a sad outcome to a mismanaged policy—and yet another case in which, when big-money interests are at stake, it's the little guys who suffer most.

Maria Alhuay in her grape fields. Ica, Peru.

With so much political unrest plaguing these three countries over the last hundred years, it goes without saying that wine and spirits have suffered, too. Revolutionary land reforms in Peru and Bolivia were particularly devastating for those countries' viticulture, from which they're only now recovering.

But the 1990s saw the beginning of a gastronomic revival in the area, particularly in Peru, spurred by the return of expatriates who had fled during the violent days and trained as chefs and sommeliers elsewhere. This, along with the cocktail revival around the world, has given rise to a new focus on quality pisco and singani and the cocktails made from them.

For many people, pisco remains a tangible, drinkable manifestation of the animosity between Peru and Chile, as inextricable from their long-standing feud as the land and resources over which they originally fought. Each country has even legally discredited the other's pisco; now, if you see Peruvian pisco in Chile, or vice versa, it's not labeled "pisco" but the more generic "aguardiente"—which could be anything. *Ouch.*

I am not going to come down on one side or another of this long-standing, complex debate. I feel I can say objectively that there are great piscos from both countries, and I find it to be far more productive to think of the two in comparison: to truly appreciate Chilean and Peruvian piscos means dropping the debate over which of them is the "real" one, and tasting both with their history and cultures in mind, while sussing out their essential stylistic differences.

For me, the comparison is a fairly simple one: Peruvian producers tend to lean more toward the rule-bound, conservative, and pointedly old-school model of pisco making, while Chileans lean a little more liberal in their production rules and thus have more room for experimentation. Viewing them this way, it's easier to see how both approaches would have their merits. Though both countries control their pisco production to a certain degree, Peru's producers certainly take the cake in that dimension. They take pride in being pisco purists, and in sticking as closely as possible to the spirit's historical origins, such as single distillation—which allows them to emphasize and perfect those aspects of pisco that they consider to be traditional and venerable. Chile, by contrast, takes a more adaptable approach to its pisco production—which allows it to push the boundaries of what exactly pisco can be. For an example of this difference, take each's approach to aging: Peru, in keeping with a traditional style, follows a strict no-wood-aging policy, whereas Chile has embraced the oak-barrel aging made popular among other spirits around the world. Obviously, both approaches can lead to good piscos, or bad; it's a question of how each is followed.

This difference in approach can also help us understand certain differences in the way the two styles of pisco are perceived and consumed worldwide. As far as basic production is concerned, it can't be argued that the more loosely regulated Chile is pumping out the juice at a rate far surpassing Peru. Though Peru boasts more than six hundred producers and Chile has just over two dozen, Chile outproduces Peru at rate of about 5 to 1, cranking out about fifty million liters of pisco a year. Chile is also the world's biggest consumer of pisco: not only do Chileans drink 90 percent of their own country's pisco but they're the world's second-largest consumer of the Peruvian stuff too, gulping down a whole 45 percent of Peru's pisco exports each year—even while making sure to import it under the generic name *destilado de uva* or *aguardiente de uva*. (Even the bitterest nationalistic debates have their limits, it seems.)

Chile's embrace of a wider range of production methods has also made its product a little more adaptable to the global spirits market. By contrast, Peru has been able to corner the premium cocktail market in recent years by branding its pisco as the more historically authentic version of the spirit— exactly the kind of thing that suspender-snapping cocktail nerds the world over like to geek out on.

Legally, both countries have DOs for their piscos. Chile beat Peru to the punch with this too, and registered its DO in 1931, regulating that the country's pisco could be made only within the marked areas of Atacama and Coquimbo. Peru created a DO in 1990, specifying that their country's pisco could be made only in areas at or below two thousand meters above sea level in Lima, Ica (including the regions of Ica, Chincha, and Pisco), Arequipa, Moquegua, and the Sama, Locumba, and Caplina Valleys of Tacna. After the drama between Chile and Peru, Bolivia got on the DO train, too, in 1988, regulating that its own grape distillate, singani, can be made only in a specific region of the high valleys surrounding the old mining town of Potosí.

Waiting to weigh and load grapes. Tarija, Bolivia.

Of course, just as with any other DO, that which restricts production brings some drama along with it; and in these three countries, anything made outside the DO-specified geographic restrictions cannot carry the names *pisco* or *singani*, but must simply be labeled as grape aguardiente. Because of this, many other worthy grape distillates from all over South America—and they're certainly out there—are barred from carrying the big important name that might get them recognized and consumed.

The flip side, however, is that in both Chile and Peru, the two countries' ministries of agriculture are responsible for regulating all of their pisco—which essentially means that neither's pisco is very well regulated at all—so people within each country are joining together to try to organize a *consejo regulardor* to do the job better. As a result of the lack of oversight, many companies are growing faster than their quality levels can keep up with—a huge problem for an industry whose future, as BarSol Pisco's Diego Loret de Mola says, "depends so much on exporting the best quality possible."

In addition to their geographic regulations, the DOs of these three countries also place different legal restrictions on the grapes they use in their spirits. In puritan Peru, the country's four different types of pisco can be made from only eight grape varietals that thrive in the country's largely arid, desert-like growing regions. (During the writing of this book, Peru was considering adding a ninth, but it hadn't happened.) Any other type of grape is strictly ruled out—if the regulators notice, that is. (A lot of producers get away with cheating the system by using reject table grapes that are too dinged-up for export. Sugar is sugar, right?) In Chile, thirteen different types of grape are allowed, but only five of these are really widely used, and some group all of the Moscatel grapes as one grape category. Both countries categorize their grapes as either "aromatic" or "nonaromatic," with Chile's (based mostly around the very aromatic Moscatel grape) being the more aromatic set overall. They disagree as to whether one grape they both use—the Torontel grape—is one or the other; to the more aromatic-heavy Chilean palate it seems less aromatic, whereas to the Peruvians it seems more so. The so-called aromatic grapes create heavier, sweeter, and more floral spirits; nonaromatics tend to produce a more diatonic distillate.

Bolivia's requirements for the grapes used in its traditional spirit are even more specific. The area of the country in which a handful of producers make all of the country's singani, a region encompassing the valleys of Tarija, Chuquisaca, Potosí, and La Paz, sits between 5,250 and 9,500 feet above sea level. (Legally, singani has to be made from start to finish at or above 5,250 feet above sea level, from the growing of the grapes to the bottling of the final distillate.) At these elevations—some of the highest viticultural regions in the world—the mountain air tends to be thin, dry, and not particularly heat-retentive, which means that though the strength of the sun is stronger during the day, the temperature drops sharply in the shade and at night, leading to broad fluctuations in temperature. These extreme daily conditions, along with equally drastic seasonal climate swings, produce hardy, extremely aromatic grapes whose flavor well reflects the tough conditions they endure. One of these tough varietals, the white-wine grape Moscatel de Alexandria, is the only grape allowed for use in producing singani.

In short, I find it to be a decent rule of thumb that Chilean piscos tend to be softer, very floral, and Moscatel-heavy in flavor and fragrance; whereas Peruvian piscos, even made according to the Peruvians' stricter rule set, seem to end up with a little more variation between floral and not. But these, of course, are relative terms. Every one of the grapes concerned is incredibly fragrant; and even an entirely nonaromatic pisco—say a Puro Quebranta from Peru (made, as the name suggests, entirely from the one grape)—is going to taste a lot like walking through a blossoming apple orchard. (It just won't be as aggressively floral as, say, a Puro Italia.)

Singani—which, because it is made only from Moscatel de Alexandria, would be considered a Puro Italia if it were made as pisco in Peru—most closely resembles Chilean piscos because, like some of them, it incorporates double distillation and uses a moscated grape, whereas the Peruvians only allow their piscos to be single-distilled.

Having shed some light on the present-day dispute over these grape spirits—and having proposed that all of them can be made well within their own stylistic parameters—let's talk a little bit about how they're made.

PERUVIAN PISCO STYLES

PURO A single varietal of grape is used (either aromatic or non-aromatic), and the must is fully fermented before distillation.

ACHOLADO A blend of varietals is used—generally both aromatic and nonaromatic—and the must is fully fermented before distillation.

MOSTO VERDE ("GREEN MUST") Pisco is distilled from partially fermented must and a single grape varietal is used (either aromatic or nonaromatic).

CHILEAN PISCO STYLES

GROUPED BY ABV (AS PER OFFICIAL CHILEAN REGULATIONS):

CORRIENTE OR TRADICIONAL 30 to 34.9 percent ABV

ESPECIAL 35 to 39.9 percent ABV

RESERVADO 40 to 42.9 percent ABV

GRAN 43 to 50 percent ABV

GROUPED BY AGE VARIANT (THE NOT-SO-OFFICIAL METHOD):

UNAGED Both aromatic and nonaromatic grapes—generally a blend of nonaromatic grapes—are used.

GUARDA Piscos are aged for at least six months but less than a year, in French or American oak barrels. Again, aromatic grapes, nonaromatic grapes, and blends are used in this type.

ENVEJECIDO Pisco is aged for at least one year in small oak barrels. Aromatic grapes, nonaromatic grapes, and blends are used (but these differences aren't of much importance, being leveled out by the influence of the oak).

PRODUCTION

In South American vineyards, as in all grape-growing regions around the world, grapevines are (generally) cultivated in an extremely organized fashion: rows and rows of them stripe the mountains and are thoughtfully cared for throughout the year. Unlike agaves and sugarcane, these plants are relatively delicate, lacking a hard husk or tough stalks to protect them from the elements, which means they demand quite a bit more agricultural attention.

The individual vines themselves age from one year to the next and can live to be more than a hundred years old. After about twenty years, the vines start to yield smaller crops, leading to more concentrated, intense-flavored wines and distillates. Different producers favor different ages of vine: the vines most highly prized by singani producer Casa Real, for example, were forty years old at the time of my visit there, while Rujero, another major singani producer, still uses vines that can be a full century older. Some of the pisco grapevines I was shown at Bodega Don Amadeo in Quilmana, Cañete, Peru, dated from 1925. For propagation, farmers graft new vines onto existing root-stock or "mother" plants, which allows them to better select for flavor, productivity, and disease resistance. (This method of propagation, along with grapevines' longevity and variability from one growing season to the next, means that grape varietals are subject to constant change and permutation, both intentional and not.)

The vines are then trained into various shapes, from free-roaming ground-grown vines to elaborate stacking T-trellises, in order to maximize their return and emphasize different flavor characteristics in different growing environments. There are few more fantastic sights than driving the fields of Bolivia, with misty mountains towering above them, or those of Peru, with the desert cliffs looming in the background.

Whole vineyards are sometimes flood-irrigated (as in the drier Peru), but drip irrigation is more commonly used; in any case, drier soil is generally better for grape cultivation, because it causes the grapes to "fight" for survival, thus concentrating and elevating their sugars more efficiently. In Bolivia—areas of which get a ton of rain and look like anyone's idea of lush farmland, with rolling green hills and valleys—this necessitates planting in the rocky, sunny areas found at higher elevations in the country's mountains. In the northern regions of Chile, and in the valleys of Peru to the north of that, the lower-altitude climate is more frequently arid and desertlike, with huge areas of enormous sand dunes, very hot sun, and not a lot of forest to shade it; so in these regions, grapes grow very efficiently.

The plants go into a sort of hibernation every winter, after which, around August before the weather starts to warm up, farmers prune back the plants to encourage them to respond vigorously to the growing season ahead. The grapes begin to appear around November, and are typically harvested in February and March. At this point, the fruit's sugars will have accumulated enough for the juice not to be too acidic, but not enough for it to lose its aromatic profile, or become overly susceptible to rot.

As mentioned before, Chile claims thirteen grapes to their production and Peru names eight; in Chile, generally Moscatel de Alexandria rules the game, whereas Peru's star player tends to be the nonaromatic Quebranta. In Bolivia, they believe (and rightly!) that they have the best location on Earth for growing the Moscatel de Alexandria, so they stick to that grape and don't bother with any other.

PERUVIAN GRAPES

AROMATIC Italia (similar to Moscatel de Alexandria), Torontel, Moscatel Negra, Albilla

NONAROMATIC Quebranta, Mollar, Negra Criollo, Uvina

CHILEAN GRAPES

Torontel

Pedro Jimenez

MOSCATEL Moscatel de Alexandria, Moscatel Rosada (Pastilla), Moscatel de Austria, Moscatel Temprana, Moscatel Amarilla, Moscatel de Canelli, Moscatel de Frontignan, Moscatel Hamburgo, Moscatel Negra, Moscatel Naranja, Chasselas Musqué Vrai

BOLIVIAN GRAPE

Moscatel de Alexandria

Eddy Pereira polishes the big copper stills of San Isidro, Caserio de Yajasi, Ica, Peru.

Ripe Uvina grapes in the aired fields of pisco Angel Negro. Zuñiga-Cañete, Lima, Peru.

ENVIRONMENTAL AND ECONOMIC ISSUES WITH GRAPES

The process by which grapes are grown and harvested hasn't changed much since they were brought over by the first European missionaries. Grape pests are persistent enemies, and pesticides have unfortunately been adopted in grape production. Today there is a movement afoot to get away from the need to spray, but it's proving a long uphill road. Nasty chemicals aren't just used to fight bugs: because wine markets abroad tend to pay higher wine prices at certain times of year, chemicals are also used by some producers to force grapes to mature at different times of year than they normally would.

Competition from other crops is another major problem for the grape industry. In part this is because, as a rule, the *campesinos* (or *chapacos*, as they're called in Bolivia) who harvest grapes are all-around farmers who don't specialize in one crop; they learn to grow whatever they can, whenever they can, so high prices among other crops can lure them away. And a lot of South American crops bring in more money than grapes: asparagus, pecans, avocados, and citrus, to name a few. Even table grapes, with broader world markets, are more profitable than grapes used for distillates; in comparison with grapes destined for pisco, table grapes can sell for more than triple the money.

Fortunately, some producers out there are working hard to do the right thing. In most cases, this simply involves developing strong relationships with grape producers; sometimes it means using a portion of the profits to pay more competitive prices for grapes. Casa Real in Tarija, Bolivia owns only 20 percent of its moscatel vineyards, a percentage the company's owners maintain in order to keep business in the hands of the families who already own and work the rest of the land they buy from. When I visited there, I also saw houses and a small school that the owners had built on-premises for their year-round workers. It's efforts like these that really demonstrate producers' commitment to their local economies.

The harvesting process is accomplished either by hand or by machine. (In Peru, pisco grapes are commonly harvested by hand, according to tradition. All singani grapes in Bolivia are also hand harvested for practical reasons: the terraced slopes where they're grown cannot be efficiently worked by machine. Chile does both.) Hand harvesting of the grapes is often done by farmers working in teams of two or three; in Bolivia I saw groups of (generally) women cutting the grapes and putting them in crates while (generally) a man ran down the rows of grapes with the filled crates—sometimes at a full-on sprint, as they're usually paid by the crate—hauling them to waiting trucks. This is hot, dusty work, and it's done from very early in the morning to about midday to avoid the sun's hottest hours.

The picked and crated grapes are then transported to a *bodega* (wine-producing house) for pressing. Traditionally pressing was a human activity—done, yes, with one's feet—but even then, it's far from most people's romantic ideal. Grape-stomping is hard work, requiring a lot of muscle and protection from the harsh acids released by the fruit; so when it's done, it's generally done not by light-stepping barefoot country damsels, but by big, strong guys in thick rubber boots. Stomping is also pretty inefficient— recovering 40 or 45 percent of the grape's juice, versus the 85 percent that machine presses can squeeze out—and it crushes the stems and seeds right along with the rest of the fruit, resulting in higher levels of methanol, more bitter tannins, and other undesirable qualities. Nowadays, for all these reasons, the pressing process is generally accomplished mechanically with various types of machine crushers, all of which are designed to impressively express the grapes while removing their seeds and stems intact. Peruvians can leave their *pomace* (the leftover skins from the pressing) in the mix for as long as they would like in their fermentation process, but generally they remove it, as do the Chileans.

Fermentation of the grape juice into wine lasts anywhere from five days (in the case of Mosto Verde or "green must" piscos of Peru, which are only partially fermented) to fifteen or twenty days. In Peru, the process is meant to be accomplished entirely with the yeasts naturally occurring on the grapes themselves, with no additional fermentation agents of any kind allowed. Fermentation in Chile is accomplished, for the most part, without any additives but sometimes some can sneak in. Bolivian singani producers are allowed to use additional yeast, but only specific patented strains.

All three countries use single-batch copper-pot stills in the production of their grape spirits. Generally the Chileans distill to between 55 and 73 percent ABV in stills that have a small rectifying column like a cognac still (also seen in rhum agricole production thanks to the French), which enable very narrow cuts of the heart from heads and tails. Producers can legally distill as many times (and to as high a proof) as they'd like in Chile, though they usually opt for the one-and-a-half-distillations that the rectifying column makes possible, and dilute the strong spirit afterward with water. (Due to this, there is quite a bit of Chilean pisco out there that is more of a grape vodka than anything else, with all of its nuance distilled out of it and a lot of water added to bring it back down to a drinkable ABV.)

The Peruvians legally allow only pot stills in the form of alembics or *falcas*, a unique design of traditional pot still that buries the still in the ground and keeps the top above, but excludes the alembic's usual bulbous swan neck. (It's like a much larger version of some of the more rudimentary Mexican stills: essentially an entombed bowl with a tube on the top to capture steam.) Peruvians can legally distill their pisco only once, but in this single distillation they're able to bring the spirit to an impressive 48 percent ABV, due to the high sugar content of their desert-grown grapes (I have even seen a 50 percent acholado from Don Amadeo!) Insanely, they do not allow adding any water to bring down the proof after distillation, instead permitting only costly evaporation to achieve the desired proof between 38 to 48 percent. Bolivian singani is never blended nor adulterated with additives; Bolivians distill their singani at least twice, and sometimes more. (I don't know why, though—the single-distilled singanis I've tasted remain my favorite, as they remain the most purely grape-y).

Legally, all of these grape-distillate producers must rest their products before bottling: for at least six months in Bolivia, for at least ninety days in Peru, and for at least sixty days in Chile. Some of the more artisanal producers elect to rest their piscos even longer; most of the producers I respect and have visited tend to have settled on two years as an appropriate time. The pisco is kept in nonreactive vessels, like glass or stainless-steel containers or traditional clay *botijas,* which allow it to mellow without taking on any of the flavors of a material such as wood.

Pisco really gets fun when you break into the Peruvian *acholado* category. Similar to Oaxacan *ensamble* production, where they mix agaves to produce complex blended mezcales, Peruvians like to blend their grapes and come up with interesting new combinations of flavor and aroma. (Not that Chile doesn't blend grapes, too, but the style is more properly Peruvian.) Also similar to mezcal *ensambles*, blended piscos used to be the norm. Frequently, the Quebranta functions in Peruvian pisco as a canvas on top of which other, more aromatic grapes (like the soft, floral Torontel, or the more acidic Italia) are painted; in different proportions to create new *acholados.*

As for why Chile ages its pisco and Peru doesn't, I've heard different theories; one of my favorites holds that when pirates came down the coast of South America to pillage and plunder, they left rum casks behind in what is now Chile, and—*ta-da!*—aged pisco was born. (And, hey, if someone out there can get me a rum cask–finished pisco, I'd be much obliged.) Singani is not traditionally aged, but there is no rule against the practice in its DO, so recent years have seen some experimentation with it.

Most Chileans use oak from Europe or the United States to age their pisco, but the law doesn't specify what kind of wood has to be used, and early records list other indigenous woods being put to the purpose. (One of these, a type of native Chilean beech called rauli, is still used.) I personally would love to see some dedication to different endemic woods being used as a point of pride in Chilean barrel-aging again, similar to what's happened with cachaça in Brazil.

While everyone likes to argue over who gets to lay claim to pisco and why, what is certain is that the spirit is finally beginning to gain a little traction again. This, as always, will have good and bad results; and as the world becomes more aware of these delicious distillates—as I can't believe it won't, in years to come—the important thing will be how well it's made in terms of quality, cultural relevance, and environmental and ethical standards.

There is a cultural terroir inherent to each country's unique grape aguardientes that represents each country's postcolonial ethics and identities. Chile, at its best, is the avant-garde contemporary, the free-thinking businessman pushing boundaries and taking its cultural productions in new directions;

at worst it's merely an industrial powerhouse, the teenage son whose only interest lies in cranking up the volume on that horrible racket he calls music. Peru, at its best, is the preservationist, the traditionalist, the reverent historian, unbending in loyalty to tradition in its pursuit of the pure; at its worst it's the hidebound old crank, listening to the racket coming from Chile's room and thinking, *What the hell has the world come to?* And Bolivia? Bolivia's the ultrafocused purist who retreated to its own tower to get really good at one thing—the beautiful stepsister who never wanted any part in this mess at all, thank you very much.

PISCO SOUR

2 oz BarSol Acholado
Peruvian Pisco

½ oz lemon juice

½ oz lime juice

¾ oz Simple Syrup
(see page 243)

½ oz egg white

4 drops Angostura
Aromatic Bitters

Morris's Bar, opened in 1916 in Lima, Peru, by American expat Victor Morris, solidified pisco's place within the world of classic cocktails with the Pisco Sour, for which Morris is credited as inventor. Morris died in 1939, at which point his many bartenders spread around the world, carrying the Pisco Sour and other great drinks with them.

At our current moment in history, the Pisco Sour is what keeps pisco on the map. This version is my own, using lemon and lime juice to attempt to mimic the flavor of the small, acidic limes of South America.

Add all the ingredients, except the Angostura Aromatic Bitters, to a cocktail shaker. Dry shake without ice to emulsify the egg white. Add ice, shake, and strain into a coupe glass. Garnish by dropping the bitters on top.

SHOTGUN WEDDING

1 oz Tea-Infused
Singani 63
(recipe follows)

¾ oz Novo Fogo
Silver Cachaça

¾ oz Vanilla Syrup
(see page 243)

¾ oz lime juice

½ oz coconut cream

½ oz coconut milk

½ oz Lustau Palo
Cortado Sherry

¼ oz Fernet Vallet Liqueur

Freshly grated nutmeg
for garnish

When I first heard of singani, I was thrilled to use it before I even tasted it. I was like, *Aha! Bolivia—another Latin country to represent at the bar!* Upon tasting it, however, I knew it would be a tricky component to work with, requiring some heavy-hitting complementary flavors to combat its heavily floral notes. Making singani drinks with other floral flavors just doesn't work: you need something for it to butt up against. After all, unity sometimes only comes through conflict!

For this drink, I decided to infuse the singani with tannic gunpowder green tea, to bite through the fat of the coconut and sweetness of the vanilla. The Mexican Fernet Vallet liqueur is rich and dark, and when mixed into the drink, it enhances the tannic tea to dry things out a little further.

Add all the ingredients, except the Fernet Vallet and the nutmeg, to a cocktail shaker with ice. Shake briefly and strain over crushed or pebbled ice in a Collins glass. Float the Fernet Vallet on top of the drink, top with a little fresh ice, and garnish with grated nutmeg.

TEA-INFUSED SINGANI 63

4 Tbsp gunpowder green tea   750 ml Singani 63

MAKES 750 ML · In a food-safe container, mix together the green tea and the singani. Allow to infuse for 20 minutes, run through a chinois strainer, and bottle. Stored refrigerated indefinitely.

LONG JUMP

¾ oz Capurro Torontel
Peruvian Pisco

¾ oz Lustau Almacenista
Palo Cortado Sherry

½ oz Plantation
Pineapple Rum

½ oz Rittenhouse
Rye Whiskey

4 dashes Rum Fire
Jamaican Rum

½ tsp Pineapple Syrup
(see page 242)

1 dash House Aromatic
Bitters (see page 241)

Orange twist for garnish

With pisco I usually think light, citrusy, and bright, but here I took the opposite approach to make a darker sipper (pictured opposite). Using the Torontel pisco with its rich jasmine notes as my starting point, I use the age and sweetness of the pineapple rum to bridge to the proof, dryness, and spiciness of the rye whiskey. The Palo Cortado sherry and just a few dashes of highly potent Jamaican rum make this a contemplative, Manhattan-like drink.

Stir all the ingredients, except the orange twist, in a mixing glass and strain into a Nick and Nora glass. Express the oils of the orange twist over the glass and then rest the twist on the rim.

FITTED ACTION

¾ oz Rujero Singani

½ oz Siembra Azul
Reposado Tequila

¾ oz Punt e Mes Vermouth

½ oz Contratto Bitter

¼ oz Vicario Savage
Cherry Liqueur

1 dash House Aromatic
Bitters (see page 241)

Maraschino cherry
for garnish

This drink was inspired by an eye-opening lunch I had in the fields of Bodegas Concepción, where Rujero Singani is made. There (over wine and singani), I learned about the history of the region, its singani traditions, and the power of this delicious spirit to raise communities out of poverty.

Add all the ingredients, except the maraschino cherry, to a mixing glass with ice. Strain over a big rock in a rocks glass. Garnish with the cherry skewered with a pick.

PISCES RISING

1½ oz BarSol Acholado
Peruvian Pisco

½ oz La Guita
Manzanilla Sherry

½ oz lemon juice

½ oz grapefruit juice

½ oz Simple Syrup
(see page 243)

½ tsp Giffard
Crème de Pêche

2 dashes Bitter Truth
Celery Bitters

1 oz soda water

Lemon wheel for garnish

Grapefruit half-wheel
for garnish

One evening in Peru, while I was driving through Ica after a long, cloudy day of rare rainfall in the arid desert vineyards, the clouds finally cleared to reveal some of the crispest, brightest stars that I've ever seen. On the opposite side of the world from where I was born in Vermont, I felt somehow at home. Yes, I'd lived momentarily in Peru when I was in college—but I'd never felt at home there. Now, on the other hand, I felt tranquil . . . totally at peace.

Pisces is the sign in the zodiac that embodies the opposite, balancing energies underlying the world. Via the stars and my feeling of balance in Ica, this drink represents that centering experience for me.

Add all the ingredients, except the lemon wheel and the grapefruit half-wheel, to a cocktail shaker with ice. Shake and strain into a Collins glass over fresh ice. Garnish with the lemon wheel and grapefruit half-wheel placed inside the glass.

TIGHT CONNECTION

¾ oz Singani 63

¾ oz jalapeño-infused Siembra Valles tequila (see page 242)

1 oz Wölffer Estate Verjus

½ oz Yellow Chartreuse

¼ oz Deniset-Klainguer Fraise des Bois

Thin cucumber slice for garnish

When I did my whirlwind South American tour in preparation for this book, traipsing around from Peru to Bolivia to Brazil, I thought, *How hard can it be? It's all one continent; I've been to all these places before.* And yet!—it turns out it's pretty damn hard to get from one remote area of one country to another. It's a journey that's not for the faint of heart—or the impatient at airports—but trust me, it's absolutely worth it!

Stir all the ingredients, except the cucumber, in a mixing glass with ice. Strain over a big ice cube in a rocks glass. Garnish with the cucumber slice.

BUENA ONDA

2 oz Yerba Mate–
Infused BarSol Italia
Selecto Peruvian Pisco
(recipe follows)

½ oz lemon juice

½ oz lime juice

¾ oz Simple Syrup
(see page 243)

½ oz egg white

1 drop Bittermans
Hopped Grapefruit Bitters

4 drops Angostura
Aromatic Bitters

When I lived in Argentina, I adopted the habit of drinking yerba mate out of the traditional dried gourd with the filtered straw. I would drink it, religiously, throughout the day. Years later I returned for the first time, this time working in the cocktail world and visiting every bar I could. I was particularly struck by a mate cocktail I tried at one of them that contrasted the tea leaves' bitterness against a sweet punch.

This cocktail builds on the simplicity of a Pisco Sour but incorporates mate for some added tannins. The result, I like to think, is pan-Latin in feel.

Add all the ingredients, except the Angostura Aromatic Bitters, to a cocktail shaker. Dry shake without ice to emulsify the egg white. Add ice, shake, and strain into a coupe glass. Garnish by dropping the Angostura bitters on top.

YERBA MATE–INFUSED BARSOL ITALIA SELECTO PERUVIAN PISCO

3 Tbsp yerba mate   750 ml pisco

MAKES 750 ML · Combine the yerba mate with the pisco in a food-safe container and let sit for 8 minutes. Fine-strain through a coffee filter and rebottle. Store in the refrigerator indefinitely.

SAN ISIDRO

1¼ oz BarSol Italia Mosto Verde Peruvian Pisco

¾ oz Clément Canne Rhum Bleue

¼ oz Suze Aperitif

¾ oz Pineapple Syrup (see page 242)

¾ oz lime juice

2 sprigs cilantro

San Isidro is the patron saint of agriculture in Catholicism. Though *campesinos* (farmers) the world over pray to this particular saint, never had I seen such devotion to him as in the Ica Valley in Peru.

I was raised in a spiritual but relatively agnostic household, and in my first journeys across Latin America, I was struck by the power of the Catholic Church: both its history of brutality in the name of God and also the current status of an entire continent arguably more dedicated than Europe is today to this faith. My first time living in Peru, I was volunteering teaching kindergarten and had to take a series of buses to get from Cuzco out of town, and every time we passed a church—there were literally dozens—everyone on every bus crossed themselves. It amazed me that it didn't matter how poor or how rich, how light-skinned or dark-skinned the people were—Catholicism tied them together.

To me, bars are the only other thing that can come close to having that kind of unifying power. This drink is a celebration of that.

Add all the ingredients, except for 1 sprig of the cilantro, to a cocktail shaker with ice. Shake and fine-strain into a coupe glass. Garnish with the remaining sprig of cilantro floating inside the glass.

PACHAMAMA

¾ oz Gilles Brisson
VS Cognac

½ oz Singani 63

½ oz Lo-Fi Gentian Amaro

¼ oz St. George
Pear Brandy

¼ oz Cynar

¾ oz Cinnamon Bark
Syrup (see page 241)

¾ oz lemon juice

½ oz egg white

1 dash Angostura
Aromatic Bitters

2 pear slices for garnish

2 cloves for garnish

Among the Incan people of the Andes, Pachamama is the goddess of fertility, the harvest, and the earth. Bolivia still maintains one of the most numerous indigenous populations in Latin America, and while Catholicism is now undisputably the religion of the country, many people continue to pray to the ancient deities.

When I was there visiting Tarija, Bolivia, I had the opportunity to go to a farming co-op the day they confirmed the sales of their harvest of Muscat de Alexandria to the singani-making house Casa Real. It was cause for celebration, and we danced, sang, and drank the day away in honor of the harvest and its rewards. This drink is a fall-time sour, celebrating the fruits of harvest and the opportunities it can bring.

Add all the ingredients, except the pear slices and the cloves, to a cocktail shaker. Dry shake without ice to emulsify the egg white. Add ice, shake, and strain into a coupe glass. Finish by fanning the pear slices and piercing the cloves through their tops to tack them together. Rest this on the side of the glass.

HEY SUZE

4 sugar snap peas

¾ oz Simple Syrup
(see page 243)

1 oz BarSol Quebranta
Peruvian Pisco

¾ oz Tanqueray Gin

½ oz Suze

¾ oz lemon juice

2 dashes absinthe

2 dashes Saline Tincture
(see page 243)

1 oz club soda

Mint sprig for garnish

4 to 5 spritzes
absinthe spray

This light, bitter drink (pictured opposite) takes a less-floral pisco and contrasts it with a big, bold juniper-heavy gin. The goal behind it was to build a drink around the sweet vegetal qualities of peas; the grape brings more sweetness to the party, and the gin and Suze add a bitter bite. A couple of dashes of absinthe highlight the vegetal character even more.

Muddle the peas in the simple syrup in a cocktail shaker. Add the remaining ingredients, except for the club soda, the mint, and the absinthe spray. Shake, fine-strain into a highball glass over fresh ice, and top with the club soda. Garnish with the mint sprig inside the glass and spritz the absinthe over the top for aromatics.

50/25/25

¾ oz La Diablada
Acholado Peruvian Pisco

¾ oz Fords Gin

1½ oz Lo-Fi Dry Vermouth

1 dash Regan's
Orange Bitters

Lemon twist for garnish

2 manzanilla olives

Pisco can find its perfect companion in gin, whose botanicals play awesomely with many piscos' floral notes. For this particular drink, I took the most iconic cocktail of all time, the martini, and gave it a split base of gin and pisco to change things up.

Add all the ingredients, except the lemon twist and the manzanilla olives, to a mixing glass with ice. Stir and strain into a martini glass. Express the oils of the lemon twist over the drink and place the twist in the glass with the olives on a cocktail pick.

POINT BEING

1¼ oz Wild Turkey Rye Whiskey

¾ oz Singani 63

¼ oz Massenez Mirabelle Plum Brandy

½ oz Lustau Moscatel Sherry

2 dashes House Aromatic Bitters (see page 241)

Orange twist for garnish

Singani 63 and Casa Real's head of production, Jorge Edgardo Furio, is not Bolivian but Argentinian, and he made it worth the long trek out to Tarija to meet him. I found his perspective on singani to be fascinating. As a winemaker, he brings a unique vision to spirits making, and even as an expatriate, he shows massive pride in the national spirit of Bolivia. "This spirit is the heart of these high mountains," he told me. "There's a pride in what we make, because it's what these people are. That's the point."

Stir all the ingredients, except the orange twist, in a mixing glass with ice. Strain over a big ice cube in a rocks glass. Express the oils of the orange twist over the glass and then place the twist inside the glass.

PISCO PONCHE

1 oz BarSol Acholado
Peruvian Pisco

½ oz ElVelo Tequila

1½ oz Tepache
(recipe follows)

¾ oz pineapple juice

¾ oz lemon juice

¾ oz lime juice

1 dash Angostura
Aromatic Bitters

The cocktail industry is a wasteful one: from the energy
it takes to fly bottles around the world to the enormous
amount of waste that bars produce. One way Shannon
Ponche and I try to combat that at Leyenda is with a house-
fermented tepache, made from the residual skins and pulp
of the pineapples we juice. The tepache can be enjoyed on
its own as a slightly fermented but essentially nonalcoholic
beverage, or enjoyed in this drink, which can easily be made
larger to serve big groups. Keep in mind that since tepache
is a fermented beverage and takes a few days to ferment, it
has to be made in advance.

**Add all the ingredients to a mixing glass with ice. Stir and
then strain over fresh ice into a wine glass.**

TEPACHE

Skins and leftover pulp from
the juicing of 1 large pineapple,
yielding about 1 qt

1 cone piloncillo or panela sugar
(You can use about 1 cup raw
sugar if you can't find panela)

3 qt water

1 tsp allspice berries

1 tsp whole cloves

5 cardamom pods

MAKES 3 QT · Combine all the ingredients in a food-safe
container and let sit unrefrigerated for 3 to 5 days, until
fermented. As the mixture begins to ferment, tiny bubbles
will form on the top and the taste will become slightly (not
very!) vinegary. Pass through a chinois strainer and then
bottle. Store in the refrigerator for up to 1 month.

CHILCANO

½ strawberry

2 oz BarSol Quebranta
Peruvian Pisco (or
Singani 63 for a Choofly)

¾ oz Ginger Syrup
(see page 168)

¾ oz lime juice

1 oz club soda

Lime wheel for garnish

Candied ginger
for garnish

Believe it or not, Peruvians were drinking pisco mules in the 1800s, long before Moscow was given its own claim to fame. This drink (pictured opposite)—called the Chilcano—is now having a revival in Peru, and it is consumed in such quantities that a new verb has been coined: *chilcaniar*, or "to chilcano." Its Bolivian cousin, the Choofly, is in effect a Singani mule.

Though the drink is usually made with ginger ale or ginger beer, I decided to spice mine up with our own ginger syrup, and took the liberty of adding richness with some strawberry.

Muddle the strawberry in a cocktail shaker. Add all the remaining ingredients, except the club soda, the lime wheel, and the candied ginger, to the cocktail shaker with ice. Shake and fine-strain into a highball glass over fresh ice. Top with the club soda and garnish with the lime wheel and candied ginger skewered together on a cocktail pick.

PISCO PUNCH

2 oz Capurro Acholado
Peruvian Pisco

1 oz pineapple juice

¾ oz lemon juice

½ oz Cane Syrup
(see page 240)

2 dashes Fee Brothers Old
Fashion Aromatic Bitters

4 whole cloves

This recipe is Julie Reiner's rendition of the classic San Francisco gold-rush cocktail. While the real recipe is up for debate (as is known in the industry, the original recipe was a secret and taken to the grave), it is generally assumed that the drink contains pisco (duh), citrus of one kind or another, pineapple, and spices of some sort. I decided to make mine with an acholado pisco—as I believe most piscos traveling around during the late eighteenth century probably were.

Add all the ingredients to a cocktail shaker with ice. Shake and fine-strain into a wine glass with a single cube of ice.

SPICY LLAMA

1½ oz El Gobernador
Chilean Pisco

½ oz Arette Blanco Tequila

¾ oz lime juice

¾ oz pineapple juice

½ oz Jalapeño Syrup
(recipe follows)

¼ oz egg white

2 dashes Bitter Truth
Celery Bitters

Edible orchid for garnish
(optional)

This drink was created by Leanne Favre, and it takes a vegetal approach to a floral Chilean pisco. The result is a fantastic, colorful drink that does an excellent job of looking like it tastes: sweet-and-spicy, grassy, with bright floral notes.

Add all the ingredients, except for the orchid, to a cocktail shaker. Dry shake without ice to emulsify the egg white. Add ice, shake, and strain into a coupe glass. If you can get an edible orchid, garnish the rim of the glass with it. (I love the bright pink of the orchid against the bright green, but it's only decoration, so if you can't get it, don't fret.)

JALAPEÑO SYRUP

5 or 6 jalapeños   2 oz agave nectar

MAKES 6 OZ · Juice the jalapeños in a juice extractor to yield about 4 oz juice. Add the agave nectar, whisk together to integrate, and bottle. Store in the refrigerator for up to 2 weeks.

FALSE ALARM

1 oz Capurro Quebranta
Peruvian Pisco

½ oz lemon juice

½ oz Raspberry Syrup
(see page 72)

¼ oz Campari

2 oz brut Champagne

3 raspberries

When I lived in Peru for a short stint in college, we drank a bright-red, sweet cola called Kola Inglesa with pisco whenever we went out. It was certainly a college student's sugary hangover delight—but when I started to dive deeper into cocktail creation, I remembered it fondly and made up this fancier version. It really only resembles the Kola Inglesa in its red appearance, as the bitterness of the Campari gives it a different flavor altogether: fresher and more nuanced.

Add all the ingredients, except the Champagne and the raspberries, to a cocktail shaker with ice. Shake and fine-strain into a wine glass with fresh ice. Top up with the Champagne and garnish with the raspberries.

PEACE TREATY

1 oz Capurro Quebranta
Peruvian Pisco

1 oz La Gitana
Manzanilla Sherry

¾ oz Waqar Moscatel
Chilean Pisco

¼ oz Vicario Olive
Leaf Liqueur

1 dash Saline Tincture
(see page 243)

1 dash House Orange
Bitters (see page 242)

Pickled caper berry
for garnish

Yeah, I did it: I put Chilean and Peruvian piscos in a drink . . . together! Really, I wanted to play around with doing my own acholado-style pisco (pictured opposite), blending the two countries' spirits to create a nice background to build upon. Taking a martini as my inspiration, I replaced the usual vermouth with a manzanilla sherry, given a little weight by olive-leaf liqueur; it represents the offering of an olive branch between the two countries.

Add all the ingredients, except the caper berry, to a mixing glass with ice. Stir and strain into a rocks glass with one large ice cube. Garnish with the caper berry resting on the ice.

FIFTH PEW

1¼ oz Singani 63

¾ oz Ancho Reyes Liqueur

¾ oz lemon juice

¼ oz maple syrup

2 dashes House Aromatic
Bitters (see page 241)

1 Tbsp black currant
compote

Lemon wheel for garnish

Chili powder for garnish

When we were in the build-out stage at Leyenda, I had the idea of using church pews for seating in our back area. (Really, calling it an idea isn't putting it quite strongly enough; I was pretty much dead-set on it.) At first, of course, we couldn't find any—and then, magically, we found four just down the street at a reused building-supply store.

The magic continued into the build-out, when we somehow gained a fifth pew. It was unaccounted for when we picked up the others: nobody has any idea how we got it or where it came from. This drink is an homage to that magical appearance.

Add all the ingredients, except the lemon wheel and chili powder, to a cocktail shaker with ice. Shake briefly and strain over crushed or pebbled ice in a tiki mug. Garnish with the lemon wheel dusted with chili powder.

A small shrine stands on the streets of Havana, Cuba.

AFTERWORD

*"How can I say this? It's this.
This is the real world."*

—**MAURICIO MAIA, EXECUTIVE SECRETARY
OF THE CÚPOLA DA CACHAÇA**

To me, the meaning of life comes via the experience of living it. The point is to absorb all we can, in the purest rendition possible. To experience something completely secure in its identity is also to feel secure in one's own; and there is peace in that. To me, being in the agave fields of Oaxaca watching a sunset, or in a sugarcane field in Jamaica for the harvest, or drinking cachaça in a Brazilian *boteco*, or being in a vineyard in Chile at daybreak with an espresso . . . all of this is to bear witness to something so unique, and so secure in its uniqueness, that one cannot help but fall in love with it.

Regarding the spirits in this book, I'm convinced that you *cannot* go to the places where these spirits are made and not feel the same absolute awe at what you encounter there as when you taste them. It's like being in front of a great artistic masterpiece, an ancient ruin of great historical context, or a natural wonder: to be in these places and taste the spirits that represent them is to be an active participant in their art.

I hope a great many of us can be so lucky as to visit some of these places in Latin America, to see and meet their vibrant cultures, beautiful landscapes, and kind people. As always, there's no substitute for firsthand experience, and I encourage everyone who has been inspired by an experience of Latin spirits to travel to one or more of the countries from which the spirits come, and spend some time with the wonderful people who make them. But as I hope I've conveyed in this book, even the armchair traveler can experience Latin America to some degree by enjoying the region's incredible spirits with an eye to their cultural heritage. These spirits, and the cocktails I've made to highlight them, are a little window into these places and these people, and they can begin to teach us what makes this region one of the most culinarily and culturally rich places on Earth.

Enjoy.

APPENDIX

Any syrups made over heat and brought to a boil can safely be kept refrigerated for up to 1 month. And any syrups made with fresh produce that have not been heated may be kept refrigerated for up to 2 weeks.

All infusions and bitters in spirits more than 40 percent ABV are indefinitely shelf stable due to their high alcohol content. But when in doubt, refrigerate!

AGAVE SYRUP

8 oz agave nectar

4 oz water

———————

MAKES APPROXIMATELY 12 OZ · Combine the agave and water in a blender and blend until fully integrated. Bottle.

CANE SYRUP

1 cup cane sugar

4 oz water

———————

MAKES APPROXIMATELY 1½ CUPS · Combine the sugar and water in a saucepan and bring to a simmer over low heat. Stir until the sugar is fully dissolved and integrated. Remove from the heat, let cool, and bottle.

CARDAMOM TINCTURE

½ cup ground cardamom pods

750 ml Polmos Spirytus Rektyfikowany or other 190 proof everclear

———————

MAKES APPROXIMATELY 750 ML (1 BOTTLE) AFTER STRAINING · Combine the cardamom and Spirytus in a food-safe container. Allow to sit unrefrigerated for 24 hours. Strain and bottle.

CINNAMON BARK SYRUP

10 g cinnamon bark (about 4 sticks, crushed)

1 cup superfine sugar

1 cup water

MAKES APPROXIMATELY 2 CUPS · Combine the cinnamon bark, sugar, and water in a saucepan and bring to a boil over medium heat, stirring so the sugar fully dissolves. Remove from the heat and let cool for 15 minutes. Run through a chinois strainer and then bottle.

DEMERARA SYRUP

1 cup Demerara sugar

4 oz water

MAKES APPROXIMATELY 1½ CUPS · Combine the sugar and water in a saucepan and bring to a simmer over low heat. Stir until the sugar is fully dissolved and integrated. Remove from the heat, let cool, and bottle.

HONEY SYRUP

8 oz honey

4 oz water

MAKES APPROXIMATELY 12 OZ · Combine the honey and water in a blender and blend until fully integrated. Bottle.

HOUSE AROMATIC BITTERS

1 oz Bitter Truth Aromatic Bitters

1 oz Fee Brothers Old Fashion Aromatic Bitters

MAKES APPROXIMATELY 2 OZ · Combine both bitters in a bowl and blend together. Rebottle.

HOUSE ORANGE BITTERS

3 oz Regan's Orange Bitters

1 oz Angostura Orange Bitters

MAKES APPROXIMATELY 4 OZ · Combine both bitters in a bowl and blend together. Rebottle.

JALAPEÑO-INFUSED TEQUILA

4 jalapeños

750 ml blanco tequila (I prefer tequila from the Tequila valley, such as Siembra Valles, Fortaleza, Arette, etc.)

MAKES APPROXIMATELY 750 ML · Remove the stems from the jalapeños. Cut the jalapeños in half and scrape the core (seeds and membranes) of two into a food-safe container. Dice the remaining jalapeños and place into the food-safe container. Add the tequila and allow to infuse for 12 to 20 minutes, depending on spice level desired. Rebottle.

Note: The recipe for the jalapeño tequila will vary because not all jalapeños are equally spicy. You need to taste it frequently to make sure it's right. Ensure your tequila is not cold, as cold tequila will not infuse properly.

PINEAPPLE SYRUP

1 pineapple, cut into 1-inch cubes to yield about 28 oz

1 qt superfine sugar

MAKES APPROXIMATELY 2 QT · Combine the pineapple and sugar in a bowl and place in refrigerator to macerate for 4 hours. Blend with an immersion blender and then strain through a colander and then through a chinois into 2-quart jar.

SALINE TINCTURE

1 Tbsp salt

2 oz water

——————

MAKES APPROXIMATELY 2 OZ • Combine the salt and water in a saucepan and bring to a simmer over low heat. Stir until the sugar is fully dissolved and integrated. Remove from the heat, let cool, and bottle.

SIMPLE SYRUP

1 cup superfine sugar

1 cup water

——————

MAKES APPROXIMATELY 2 CUPS • Combine the sugar and water in a saucepan and bring to a simmer over low heat. Stir until the sugar is fully dissolved and integrated. Remove from the heat, let cool, and bottle.

VANILLA SYRUP

1 vanilla bean

1 cup superfine sugar

1 cup water

——————

MAKES APPROXIMATELY 2 CUPS • Cut the vanilla bean in half and scrape the seeds into a saucepan. Add the remaining pod and the sugar and water to the pan and bring to a simmer over low heat. Stir until the sugar is fully dissolved and integrated. Remove from the heat and let cool for 20 minutes. Pour through a chinois strainer and then bottle.

ABOUT THE AUTHOR

Ivy Mix has been recognized as one of the most renowned bartenders in the world. She owns Brooklyn bar, Leyenda, which was nominated for the James Beard Award for Outstanding Bar Program in 2019 for its dedication to Latin American spirits and cocktails. She also has won the Spirited Award for American Bartender of the Year at Tales of the Cocktail and was named *Wine Enthusiast's* "Mixologist of the Year." Additionally, she co-founded Speed Rack, a bartending competition for women that raised money for breast cancer research and prevention. She lives and works in Brooklyn, NY.

ACKNOWLEDGMENTS

This book would not have been possible without the help and support of many amazing people, upon whom I relied for their skills, knowledge, hospitality, and understanding.

First and foremost, I must thank my team, my ride-or-dies: James Carpenter, who helped craft this book beyond my own feeble writing attempts, and Shannon Sturgis, whose photography skills are unmatched. We traveled, the three of us, for months for this book and it is just as much theirs as it is mine. A big thanks to Ten Speed Press for their work with me here, and to literary agency Inkwell for their support. Additionally, a huge thank-you to Emily Timberlake, for her editing and cheerleading skills.

I was only able to access the incredible places and people in this book with the help of many others, to whom I am infinitely grateful: Justin Lane Briggs, William Scanlan, Asis Cortés, Audrey Hands, Misty Kalkofen, Carlos Camarena, Stefano Francavilla, Kate Perry, Ben Jones, Joy Spence, Diego Loret de Mola, Jonathan Brathwaite, Nicolas Granier, Dragos Axinte, Luke McKinley, Mauricio Maia, Isadora Bello Fornari, Thyrso Camargo, David Suro, JP Caceres, Pedro Jiménez Guirria, and Juan Fernando Gonzalez. (I'm sure there are others I'm leaving out—and if you're one of them, thank you!) I'm also grateful to my business partners and management team at Leyenda, who kept the ship afloat during my travels—Susan Fedroff, Julie Reiner, Christine Williams, Tom Macy, Jessie Wohlers, and Shannon Ponche—and to Lynnette Marrerro and Becky Nadeau for ensuring Speed Rack would have successful events even in my absence. Last, thank you to my family—Sissy, Mom, Dad, and Gaelen McKee—and friends for keeping me sane in the depths of writing and editing.

INDEX

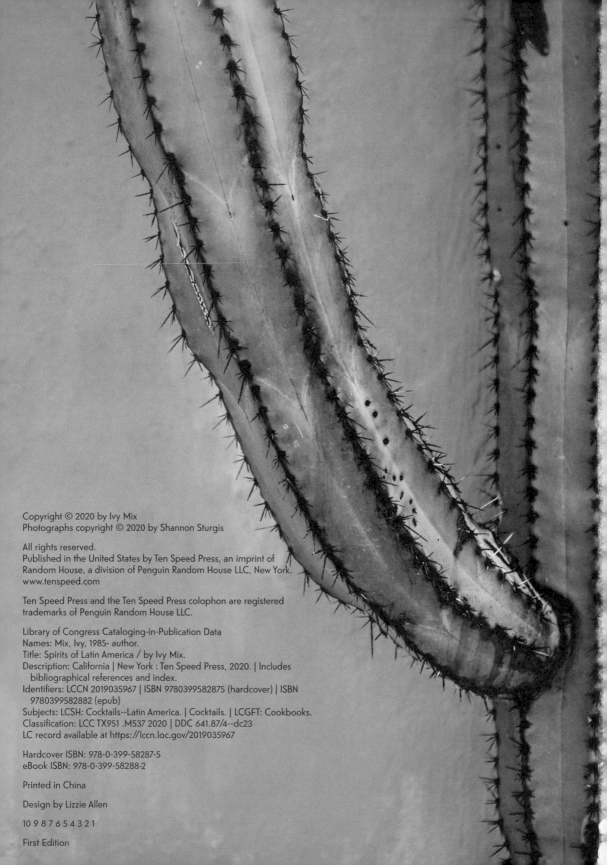

Published in the United States by Ten Speed Press, an imprint of
Random House, a division of Penguin Random House LLC, New York.
www.tenspeed.com

Ten Speed Press and the Ten Speed Press colophon are registered
trademarks of Penguin Random House LLC.

Library of Congress Cataloging-in-Publication Data
Names: Mix, Ivy, 1985- author.
Title: Spirits of Latin America / by Ivy Mix.
Description: California | New York : Ten Speed Press, 2020. | Includes
   bibliographical references and index.
Identifiers: LCCN 2019035967 | ISBN 9780399582875 (hardcover) | ISBN
   9780399582882 (epub)
Subjects: LCSH: Cocktails--Latin America. | Cocktails. | LCGFT: Cookbooks.
Classification: LCC TX951 .M537 2020 | DDC 641.87/4--dc23
LC record available at https://lccn.loc.gov/2019035967

Hardcover ISBN: 978-0-399-58287-5
eBook ISBN: 978-0-399-58288-2

Printed in China

Design by Lizzie Allen

10 9 8 7 6 5 4 3 2 1

First Edition